**WITHDRAWAL**
Mohammad Al Attar


**603**
Imad Farajin


**DAMAGE**
Kamal Khalladi


**THE HOUSE**
Arzé Khodr


**EGYPTIAN PRODUCTS**
Laila Soliman

# PLAYS FROM
# THE ARAB WORLD

MOHAMMAD AL ATTAR ■ WITHDRAWAL
Translated by Clem Naylor

IMAD FARAJIN ■ 603
Translated by Hassan Abdulrazzak

KAMAL KHALLADI ■ DAMAGE
Translated by Houda Echouafni

ARZÉ KHODR ■ THE HOUSE
Translated by Khalid Laith

LAILA SOLIMAN ■ EGYPTIAN PRODUCTS
Translated by Khalid Laith

Edited and with a Foreword by Elyse Dodgson
Introduced by Laila Hourani

BRITISH
COUNCIL

NICK HERN
BOOKS

ROYAL COURT
THEATRE

www.britishcouncil.org   www.nickhernbooks.co.uk   www.royalcourttheatre.com

**A Nick Hern Book**

*Plays from the Arab World* first published in Great Britain in 2010 as a paperback original by Nick Hern Books Limited, 14 Larden Road, London W3 7ST, in association with the British Council and the Royal Court Theatre, London

*Withdrawal* copyright © 2010 Mohammad Al Attar,
Translation copyright © 2010 Clem Naylor

*603* copyright © 2010 Imad Farajin
Translation copyright © 2010 Hassan Abdulrazzak

*Damage* copyright © 2010 Kamal Khalladi
Translation copyright © 2010 Houda Echouafni

*The House* copyright © 2010 Arzé Kohdor
Translation copyright © 2010 Khalid Laith

*Egyptian Products* copyright © 2010 Laila Soliman
Translation copyright © 2010 Khalid Laith

Foreword copyright © 2010 Elyse Dodgson
Introduction copyright © 2010 Laila Hourani

The author and translators have asserted their moral rights

Cover designed by Ned Hoste, 2H
Cover image © 2010 Photos.com, a division of Getty Images

Typeset by Nick Hern Books, London
Printed and bound in Great Britain by CLE Print Ltd, St Ives, Cambs PE27 3LE

A CIP catalogue record for this book is available from the British Library

ISBN 978 1 84842 097 7

**FSC**
The mark of responsible forestry
TT-COC-003115
FSC Trademark © 1996 Forest Stewardship Council A.C

**Contents**

## Acknowledgements

The British Council and the Royal Court Theatre would like to thank the following for all their support and commitment to this project: all the writers, translators, readers, directors and actors who have taken part in this project throughout the region and at the Royal Court from 2007–09; Laila Hourani, Carole McFadden, Rebecca Hinton, Sarah Ewans, Paul Doubleday, Shaza Kandakji, Mirvat Haddad; the British Council Arts Managers: Issam Jarash and Nisreen El Halabi (Syria), Fatme Masri and Rola Ziadeh (Lebanon), Reem Dawani (Jordan), Suha Khuffash and Merna Kassis (Palestinian Territories), Nairy Avedissian (Egypt), Imed Belekhodja, Amel Rehaiem and Ines Zaibi (Tunisia), and Hicham El Kebbaj, Farah Fawzi and Ibtissame Berrado (Morocco); Amal Bakry (the project's Audiences and Communications Manager); Dominic Cooke, April De Angelis, David Greig, Mike Bartlett, Clare Lizzimore, Hettie Macdonald, Sacha Wares, Ramin Gray, Chris James and William Drew; The Genesis Foundation who supports the ongoing work of the Royal Court International Playwrights Programme.

## Foreword

In April 2007 the British Council and the Royal Court Theatre in London embarked on a unique project working with young Arab writers across seven countries from the Near East to North Africa. Twenty-one emerging playwrights from Egypt, Jordan, Lebanon, Morocco, Palestine, Syria and Tunisia travelled to Damascus to work with the playwrights April De Angelis, David Greig and myself. There, we started a journey that spanned two years, with different phases of the work continuing in Tunis, Cairo, Amman and Beirut. I have been coordinating and leading workshops with international playwrights for the Royal Court for over fifteen years, but never has an international new-writing project been more ambitious or far-reaching.

Our first work with writers in the region began in Palestine in 1998 with a workshop for local playwrights in collaboration with Al Kasaba Theatre. Throughout the last ten years this work has continued with British writers and directors working in the West Bank, and Palestinian writers taking part in projects at the Royal Court. All of this work has been supported by the Genesis Foundation and the British Council. In 2005 the playwright David Greig began working in Syria, leading a group of playwrights there in a project initiated by the British Council. By 2006 they asked the Royal Court to become involved, too, and that culminated in a week of play-development work with Syrian writers at the Royal Court, presented in January 2007, and the participation of three Syrian writers on the Royal Court International Residency.

The next step seemed even more extraordinary. We were approached by Carole McFadden, the Drama and Dance Adviser of the British Council in London, and Laila Hourani, Regional Arts Manager for the Near East and North Africa, to participate in a new-writing project that would involve young playwrights across the whole region. This seemed to be a great opportunity that no one at the Royal Court could resist. We really had to start at the beginning as we had never worked on a regional project before. The associate directors Ramin Gray, Sacha Wares and I travelled to all of the countries and came back with different experiences and different recommendations. It was clear that some countries had much stronger theatre cultures than others and different degrees of new writing. We also had to consider the different dialects of Arabic when we were looking to translate the work. We decided, in the end, to open applications to all writers in the seven countries under the age of thirty-five and asked them to send samples of their work as well as proposals for new plays. We chose twenty-one writers and by a small miracle managed to get them all to Damascus for the first workshop. We discovered that we would be working in a beautiful ancient Damascene house in the Old City. It is difficult to describe how moving it was, after these months of travelling and planning, to come face to face with such a group of inspiring young writers in the open courtyard of this wonderful house.

It was challenging from the beginning, and some of the writers were both tentative and doubtful as they began to explore the possibilities of writing a new contemporary play for us. The only way we could change that was by concentrating on the work itself. David Greig told the writers: 'This work at its best is a dance between the side of you that dreams and the side engaged in the world.'

Three months after the first meeting, twenty out of twenty-one writers submitted drafts of new plays. In Tunis in November 2007 we helped to move the plays forward to another draft. In Cairo in March 2008 we were joined by Royal Court Artistic Director, Dominic Cooke, and invited actors from the region to take the plays to a more finished draft, which was presented to a local audience. It was difficult to make a selection of the plays to present at the Royal Court in London in November 2008, but we finally chose seven plays and presented them in a season called *I Come From There: New Plays from the Arab World*. Houses were full and there was no doubt that the very idea of this work was inspiring our British audiences too.

After further workshops with a group of regional directors, the plays began to take off in the countries of origin. Readings took place in Beirut, Amman and Tunis in 2009. In May 2009 two different plays opened on the same day in Ramallah and Damascus. I believe this is just the beginning of some extraordinary work that will be produced by new writers in the Arab world.

*Elyse Dodgson*
*Associate Director/Head of International Department*
*Royal Court Theatre*

## Young Arab Playwrights and the Half-open Door

The idea of working with Arab playwrights to develop their playwriting skills emerged when I attended the British Council showcase at the 2003 Edinburgh Festival Fringe. It was my first close experience of new British theatre. The festival that year featured hit plays like *The People Next Door* by Henry Adams, *Dark Earth* by David Harrower and *San Diego* by David Greig. I was struck by the new Scottish playwrights and their experience, and felt a commonality with the Arab world that I couldn't quite articulate at the time. Was it the 'dark earth' in David Harrower's play that reminded me of the volcanic black earth that is so characteristic of my husband's village in Sweida, south of Syria? Or was it the subtle poetry of David Greig's language that made me see the potential of the Arabic stage using an Arabic language rooted in the street, while maintaining the magic of its mother tongue? Was it the hidden feel of history and its heavy shadow on the present? Or was it the dilemma of neighbouring a strong enemy of the past?

I returned to Syria filled with the desire to follow these threads, and found myself reflecting on the current state of Arab theatre, and where an exposure to the Scottish experience could take it. This was at a time when more and more young people were searching for ways to express themselves through theatre. It was also a time that saw the emergence of numerous theatre groups mostly working on the basis of what they called 'improvisation'. Some of it was improvisation with the body – hence the emergence of dance and physical theatre companies. The other was improvisation around existing texts from the repertoire of international theatre: Shakespeare, Beckett, Brecht, Jean Genet, and so on. Rarely was there a new Arabic written text; rarely was there a written documentation of the improvisation. The theatrical experience ended with the last performance of a play. It was as if there was a fear of approaching the written word, formulating a full text, documenting a moment by writing it down.

For this young generation, words had become so associated with the words of the imam's Friday speech, or the words of the political despot, or those of the political party leader trying to oppose the despot. Words that did not speak the language that these young people used in their daily lives. Words that gave answers rather than raised questions. But these young people were boiling over with questions: questions on their identity in a fast-changing world; on the broken dreams – be they nationalist or Communist – of their parents; questions about the 'Western other', whom they started to see more of through satellite channels and the internet penetrating their homes; questions about their teachers and professors who suddenly seemed so out of date to them; questions on whether to make love or go to the mosque; whether to remain unemployed or leave the country; whether to fight for Palestine or forget about it. They were all questions that didn't find their way to the stage they longed for.

This young generation was emerging on the theatre scene after over a decade which had seen almost no fresh blood in Arab theatre. The mid-eighties to late nineties was perhaps a period of disillusion for Arabic theatre, when the eager search for the unique voices that characterised the sixties and seventies had faded completely. During those earlier decades the hot questions were over whether Arabic theatre should use standard or colloquial language, should revive traditional forms of storytelling or adopt European forms, and should remain elitist or reach out to wider audiences. But these concerns had died away unanswered, as did the dream for independent, developed and democratic states. Now we were in a time when the first Gulf War had reminded everyone in the Arab world of some recent colonial history which there hadn't been a moment to be reconciled with. It was a time when neither the Intifada nor the peace process in Palestine seemed to be bringing the region anywhere near healing this old wound. And a time when 'the fight against terrorism' swept away any hopes of reconciling the old love/hate relationship between West and East.

In my capacity as Arts Project Manager for the British Council in Syria, I proposed a new-writing project to my colleague Carole McFadden at our Drama and Dance Department in London. We invited the playwright David Greig to Damascus to deliver workshops to the students of the Theatrical Studies Department at the High Institute of Drama, one of the few formal drama schools in the Arab region. At that time, we had no idea that, from these origins, would develop a two-year project resulting in nine Syrian plays, and a long and very fruitful collaboration with Elyse Dodgson at the Royal Court Theatre in London, leading to another twenty plays from seven Arab countries, five of which are published in this collection.

The Arabic playwrights participating in the project had a long journey to take with the British playwrights David Greig and April De Angelis before reaching the plays in the form you will read them here. The journey began by building trust and assuring the Arab playwrights that the project was not about shaping their writing to fit some fixed 'UK formula'. Nor was it about treating them like one 'Arab lot', with no recognition for the diversity within the region. It was rather about sharing with them the tools that would help them find their own unique voice. And unique are the voices you will hear in these plays.

*

Hadia and Gasir, the young characters in Laila Soliman's *Egyptian Products* (Egypt), are struggling to communicate, to reach out for each other, to break out from being trapped in their memories of a dead mother (in Gasir's case) or the attachment to an old male 'Master' (in Hadia's). While Hadia and Gasir seem so representational of a young Arab generation strangled with sexual repression, the inability to break away from the past, the social pressures imposed by expectations around marriage, children and so on, they are also very much their own selves as unique characters living in the big, busy, occasionally aggressive Cairo of today. The strong sense of the city that is felt in the play – despite it mostly taking place in closed rooms – is a reflection of the diversity that each of the plays in this volume brings to the reader, despite their all rotating in a common Arabic sphere.

Likewise in Mohammad Al Attar's *Withdrawal* (Syria), a sense of Damascus is strongly felt through the single, closed room where the play takes place. But unlike Hadia and Gasir in *Egyptian Products*, young Ahmad and Nour in *Withdrawal* do not need to struggle to find a place to meet. They have rented a flat in Damascus where they are free to sleep with each other whenever they want – or so they think. They cannot stay the night together because Nour is not allowed to spend the night out; Ahmad has to go back to his family. Neither can they escape the eyes of their neighbours, who question their living together before marriage. Can they break away from these ties? Will Ahmad leave the country, or will the five minutes before the car picks him up for the airport make him stay?

This sense of entrapment, coupled with a glimpse of a door opening, someone hesitantly trying to get out, and our not knowing whether they will make the step out or not, is indeed characteristic of all the plays. Perhaps nothing reflects the desperation associated with it better than Kamal Khalladi's *Damage* (Morocco), which speaks of the near impossibility of escape. Set in a completely different part of the Arab world, where a mixture of strong African influence and long-term French colonisation adds another unique flavour to this mosaic of plays. The play beautifully takes us on the journey of a newly-wed

Moroccan couple, Youssef and Sana'a, from the blossoming of love in their home in Meknes to the landmines in the Congo that place Youssef for ever in a wheelchair.

In placing young couples at the heart of their work, these three playwrights ask questions about what it means to be a man and a woman in a masculine society. The men in these plays are not the macho men that are stereotypically anticipated in these societies. Even Youssef, who is so determined to respond to the army's call to be a soldier in the Congo, eventually reveals to his wife his vulnerability, love and desperation.

Arzé Khodr in *The House* (Lebanon) sheds another light on what it means to be a man in a masculine society. Nabeel, the only brother to two sisters who have now been deprived of their mother as well as their father, is hesitant, indecisive, totally incapable of taking a stance – just the opposite of what you would expect from someone who in Arabic societies is looked up to as 'the man of the house'. Those who are capable of determining the direction of things are the two female sisters, Nadia and Reem. The metaphor of the dilemma of selling – or not selling – the family home is very reflective of the Lebanese dilemmas of a past associated with war, destruction and fear, and of a future full of mixed feelings about rebirth versus guilt linked with denial.

Khodr's characters are trapped between the walls of their family house, while those in Imad Farajin's *603* (Palestine) are trapped within the walls of one of the most renowned Israeli prisons, Askalan. There is no question about them wanting to get out, but will they ever do so? While they all fantasise about being released from prison, only one of them actually makes his way to liberty by escaping, leaving the question for the remaining three open: 'What exactly are we waiting for?'

It's a question that perhaps all the plays in this volume voice in one way or another.

*Laila Hourani*
*Regional Manager Creativity*
*Near East and North Africa Region, British Council*

# WITHDRAWAL

انسحاب

MOHAMMAD AL ATTAR

*translated by*

CLEM NAYLOR

## Mohammad Al Attar

Mohammad Al Attar studied English Literature at the University of Damascus and has a diploma in Theatre Studies from the Higher Institute of Dramatic Arts in Damascus. In 2008 he was coordinator of the Arab and International Performing Arts programme for the Damascus Arab Capital of Culture Festival. He is currently taking an MA in Applied Drama at Goldsmiths, University of London. Since 2006 he has been a member of the Theatre Studio Group in Damascus, working as dramaturg on the Boal-inspired project *Interactive Theatre in Syrian Rural Areas* (2006–07); *Samah* (May 2008) at El Teatro, Damascus, a play performed by a group of young offenders from the Damascus Juvenile Institute; and *Al-Merwad Wa Al-Mekhala* (May 2009) at the Syrian Opera House. He was also dramaturg for a production of *An Enemy of the People* by Ibsen at the Syrian Opera House.

## Clem Naylor

Clem Naylor graduated with a BA in Arabic and French from St John's College, Oxford, in 2009. As part of his degree he spent 2006–07 studying Arabic at the University of Damascus. Since returning to the UK, he has been involved in various literary and non-literary translation projects. These projects have included work for the Royal Court Theatre, London, for whom he has translated and reported on scripts, and for the Georg Eckert Institute in Germany, for whom he translated a volume of essays about education. He is currently studying for a Modern Middle Eastern Studies MSt at Oxford and has recently returned from a British Council literary translation workshop in Cairo.

*Withdrawal* was first performed as a rehearsed reading as part of the *I Come From There: New Plays from the Arab World* season in the Jerwood Theatre Upstairs, Royal Court Theatre, London, on 12 November 2008, with the following cast:

| | |
|---|---|
| AHMAD | Sam Crane |
| NOUR | Jemima Rooper |
| *Director* | Amy Hodge |

The play was also read at Espace El Teatro in Tunis, Tunisia, in February 2009.

## Characters

AHMAD, *a twenty-six-year-old man*
NOUR, *a twenty-six-year-old woman*

## Setting

A medium-sized room with a bed taking up one side of it.
Nearby, there is a small table. Roughly in the middle of the
room, there is a table with two traditional wooden chairs around
it. Near the table, against the back wall there is a big sofa and
directly above this sofa there is a relatively big window. A large
old cupboard, which is handmade and decorated with mother-
of-pearl, occupies a large part of the second side of the room,
facing the bed. Opposite the door to the room, there is a door
leading to a small bathroom, next to which there is a very small
kitchen in the corner. We also see some unopened cardboard
boxes in the room, with small household objects, books, CDs
and various other things inside.

**Scene One**

*Night-time.* AHMAD *and* NOUR *are lying on the only mattress in the room.*

AHMAD. Maybe it's time now.

NOUR. That was so good. It was the best I've ever had.

AHMAD. It was the first I've ever had... What time is it?

NOUR. Thank you for waiting until now for me. I wanted to, too.

AHMAD. I've got to get up, he could be here any minute now.

NOUR. I really wanted to – I love you more than I've ever loved anyone before.

AHMAD. Me too... though I've never loved anyone before. I'm really going to miss you.

NOUR *grabs hold of him by his hair and pulls him forcefully towards her chest.*

NOUR. Don't joke. You can't really want to go away, not after we struggled so long to be able to rent this room. You can't go. You're going to stay with me and I'm going to sleep with you every day until you forget about all our problems.

AHMAD (*pulling himself out of her grasp*). Where's my watch? He's got to get here now so I can go home and get my things. My family will be waiting to say goodbye, my mum will be crying like usual. I'll miss her too. You and her, just you two.

NOUR (*hugging him around his shoulders from behind*). You're not really going to go, are you? You always said you weren't going to go. You're not being serious.

AHMAD. You've never taken what I say seriously. Maybe it's better like that – you know, you, my dad, my whole family, no one takes me seriously. I'll miss you.

NOUR. Liar… You're not going to go, you want to stay with me. Come on, let's do it again.

AHMAD. It's funny how I've waited my whole life for this moment… I can't quite believe this is happening.

NOUR. I wanted to wait for you too. You can't go… Not now I've found you.

AHMAD. Does your neck still hurt? You should stop sitting in front of a computer so much, eight hours a day really is too long. Maybe you should quit your job. Why don't you put on some music?

*AHMAD stands up and starts looking for his watch. Then he finds his mobile and looks at the time on it.*

NOUR (*lying on her front on the bed*). I feel like I want to cry. Please don't have a go at me.

AHMAD. No, I want to have a go at you. Don't cry, I've told you a hundred times not to cry. He should be here any minute now.

*He approaches her again and sits down on the bed.*

Everything'll be fine. It won't get any worse, anyway.

*A knock on the door.*

I told you he was about to get here. I've got to get out quickly, I don't want to keep him waiting. He's going to take me home and then on to the airport.

*He approaches her and hugs her tightly.*

NOUR. No, stay a bit longer. Let me put on the music.

*She rushes towards the CD player, but she freezes when there is another knock on the door.*

**Scene Two**

NOUR. It's the best room we could get for our money.

AHMAD. You mean, your money.

NOUR. What's the difference?

AHMAD. Just that you've got a job and I don't.

NOUR. It's stupid, you could have a job if you wanted one. You leave all your jobs because they're taking advantage of you or they don't understand you or they don't appreciate you or they –

AHMAD. You sound like someone I know.

NOUR. It was your choice. Now you're focusing more on your writing, you're getting published in a few magazines.

AHMAD. When I woke up this morning I couldn't even say good morning to him. I don't know why, it just felt like it didn't matter. I never seem to want to say anything at home, anyway.

NOUR. Oh, by the way, Leila read your last article. She said she really liked it. She wanted me to tell you.

AHMAD. Thank her for me.

NOUR. You can write without any distractions here. At least here there's a bit of peace and quiet; and then there's the view, it's so pretty in the evening, you can see half of Damascus and all the lights are on.

AHMAD. You're right, it's prettier at night. Damascus hides all its flaws at night-time. The guy who rented us this place wasn't straight with us – he didn't tell us we're next door to a school. I realised when I arrived this morning and the children were chanting the Party slogans. All the time they were chanting away, the headmistress was shouting at them. There's no way they could have understood a word of what they were saying.

NOUR. I love you.

AHMAD. Suddenly all my memories of school came back to me. I remembered what it was like to be their age.

NOUR. Do you really love me?

AHMAD. I felt like writing. I tried and kept on trying but I couldn't. I got fed up of rummaging around in my memory. I think I must have been scared.

NOUR. Why me? Why did you decide that I should be your first?

AHMAD. Maybe I should never have tried. I'm still tired. Anyway, I knew you'd be starving when you got here so I made you something to eat.

NOUR. I love you.

### Scene Three

NOUR. We've had this room for a few days now but I'm still not seeing very much of you.

AHMAD. I'm sorry. I have to stay at home a lot – Mum's ill and even if I'm not by her side all the time, I still have to be at home. Anyway, I haven't told them I'm renting a room yet. I have a feeling they'd be pretty angry.

NOUR. Maybe you never will tell them. I know how it is…

AHMAD. I called up to ask how she was just now and my dad picked up, I didn't tell him where I was. He told me to stop wasting my time and come home, do something useful, especially seeing as Mum's ill. Then he told me how I'd left my music on in my room. He hung up straight away when he got a call on his mobile from my big brother in Dubai. My brothers, both of them, are constantly calling from Dubai to ask how Mum's doing. She starts crying and saying things like 'God bless you' and 'Don't worry yourselves about me' and 'Don't waste your money calling, I'm all right', then she looks towards me and I can just tell that she pities me.

NOUR. Didn't you say you'd show me some pictures of your brothers? Are they better-looking than you?

AHMAD. They're better-looking and cleverer and, and my dad never stops talking about them and feeling sorry for me for how young I am and reminding me how my brothers have made their way in life and how they've got children. Today, when he hung up, something struck me. Listen to this – every single time he sees me or speaks to me about anything, he just has to point something out or give me a piece of advice or start preaching to me about something. Isn't that amazing? It's unbelievable! I swear – every single time.

NOUR. My dad hardly even talks to me and all my mum ever does is have a go at me.

AHMAD. I'm thinking of writing them down, counting how many of his observations he makes per day or something.

NOUR. It was always her who used to encourage me to do everything to begin with, but when things go wrong she never takes any responsibility for it.

AHMAD. Do your family still ask you about me?

NOUR. No, I told them I don't see you any more.

AHMAD. And they believe you, just like that? People can be so stupid sometimes. Anyway, I don't have anything against them. They just decided to hate me for no apparent reason.

NOUR. I think we've been through this enough times already. You didn't behave in the right way.

AHMAD. I think it's probably time I went home.

NOUR. You could have had a good relationship with my dad if you'd paid attention to what I said.

AHMAD. I'd have had to play the role of the new son in their modern family. One set of parents is quite enough for me, to

be honest… I really have to go and look after my mum,
she'll be getting upset that I'm not there.

NOUR. Stay… I thought we were going to eat together.

AHMAD. I've got to go.

NOUR. Why do I miss you so much, even with you by my side?

AHMAD. Bye.

### Scene Four

NOUR. I've had enough of the room being like this, we've had
it for a week now and we haven't done anything to it.

AHMAD. It's fine like this.

NOUR. We didn't rent it for it to be like this. Let's put some of
our things up, you know, make it a bit nicer.

NOUR *heads towards one of the cardboard boxes on the
ground and rummages around in it a bit before taking out
some paintings and photos.*

I'm going to do it up the way I like it – with pictures and
candles and I want to buy some curtains to put up instead
those tatty old ones… Burgundy curtains.

AHMAD. Burgundy?

NOUR. That's right, I like burgundy and it'll go well with the
colour of the room. I know what I'm talking about.

AHMAD. That's strange, I didn't realise this room had a colour.

NOUR *is carrying several pictures, she wanders around the
room a bit before settling on a place to hang one of them.*

NOUR. It needs a lot of work, this room. I'll just put up a few
paintings and photos for now. What do you think? Which
photo? Or should I put up some paintings?

AHMAD. I don't know.

NOUR. Okay, I'll save you the trouble and put up some of my photos, even though I know you don't think I'm a good photographer.

AHMAD. Do whatever you like.

NOUR. I'll put that photo of Damascus I took from Maya's roof in Muhajireen up here. I really like it… The light's so nice, the sky was half-covered with clouds. Opposite, over there above your head, I'll put that picture of us when we were in Ma'aloula. That was our first trip outside Damascus together. I love that photo, it reminds me of when nothing was impossible for us, the world was in our hands.

AHMAD. Great.

NOUR. And that's just the start, some time soon I'll have to find time to sort out the whole room.

AHMAD. Brilliant.

NOUR. What's wrong with you? Is something the matter?

AHMAD. No, nothing… I'm just thinking about those burgundy curtains.

**Scene Five**

NOUR. Sleepy?

AHMAD. Yes, even though I've been sleeping a lot.

NOUR. I'm sleeping less and less. Work's long then as soon as I finish I come here to spend time with you.

AHMAD. That's why you look tired.

NOUR. Do I really? Or maybe it's just that you've started to see my flaws. How long have we known each other?

AHMAD. Four years at least.

NOUR. No, I meant known each other properly.

AHMAD. Oh, less than two months. But I've liked you for ages, from when we were at university. You never even noticed me and I always used to see you moving from one guy to the next.

NOUR. No, I did notice you, but you never did anything. I admired you from afar but I wasn't brave enough to make the first move. Why didn't you take the initiative? You would have saved us a lot of time and made things a lot easier for me.

AHMAD. Today one of our neighbours stopped me, he wanted to get me into a conversation. I knew what he wanted – he clearly wanted to ask me about you and about us and about how we come here together so often. He was being unbearably friendly.

NOUR. I think I know the one.

AHMAD. There was no way I could match his friendliness. First, I was overcome by a sudden desire to hit him, then, a moment later, I felt like I wanted to throw up on him, then, when I saw his little daughter coming out of the front door and grabbing hold of his leg, I turned round and walked off. I've got a feeling him and the other neighbours are going to start making trouble soon.

NOUR. But we haven't even been renting the room for ten days and I only come for a little while every day. Well, it doesn't bother me, they can do whatever they like. Come on then, come a bit closer to me, I want to have you here.

AHMAD. Ten days? It doesn't feel like that long, it's gone so quickly. Are you going to sleep here tonight?

NOUR. I can't, what could I say to my family? We could do something now, though, I really want to.

AHMAD. And I want us to spend the night together.

NOUR. Stop running away from me, come here.

AHMAD. I hate them.

NOUR. Okay then, I'll come to you.

AHMAD. Your family.

NOUR (*sitting on* AHMAD*'s knees*). Don't you want me?

*He smiles and pushes her away gently.*

AHMAD. And my family, and the neighbours and everyone. I hate them all.

*NOUR stands up and smiles sadly.*

NOUR. Me too… But I love you, just you.

## Scene Six

NOUR. Sorry I'm so late, the traffic in town is unbelievable. It takes me a whole hour to get to you. There I was, thinking that this place was in the ideal location, not too far away.

AHMAD. The whole of Damascus is far away.

NOUR. From what?

AHMAD. Nour, you're losing weight.

NOUR. People were saying that at work today. I don't know, I'm not sleeping well and I've completely lost my appetite.

AHMAD. Maybe you're in love?

NOUR. You think? Anyway, today the manager came by our department. He said last month's work was superb and we wouldn't go unrewarded for it.

AHMAD. Great.

NOUR. It really is, and he told me specifically that he was really happy with what I was doing. He said if I carried on like this I'd have a very bright future with the company.

AHMAD. Brilliant. What exactly does a bright future mean for a journalism graduate like you? Covering more weddings and cocktail parties and receptions?

NOUR. I knew you'd react like this, you never stop going on about it.

AHMAD. You know what, when you told me the age of the owner of the company, I mean, that he was in his mid-thirties, I spent a whole day thinking about it. He's meant to be a completely self-made man. To be able to have a company of that size, he must have had to start saving up his pocket money when he was ten. Sometimes he must have skipped meals to avoid spending. I mean, he was clearly getting more and more pocket money as he got older, but only within reason – his father was a very important official and he was a self-made man too and he would only have given him just enough to get by on. It was then that I realised how much of an idiot I was and how I'd wasted my pocket money for so many years.

NOUR. You're like a broken record. I've told you a hundred times it has nothing to do with me. It doesn't bother me what this guy did with his life. Whether he studied or not, whether he had to work hard or not, maybe his father helped him... No, of course his father helped him, but that's just how this country works. Can't you see that? You know full well this is the best job I can get.

AHMAD. Of course it is... Writing about parties and important cocktail evenings.

NOUR. I'm going.

AHMAD. Where to? The party the company organised for tomorrow?

NOUR. I'm tired. I want to go home. Who told you about the party, anyway?

AHMAD. You did. Did you forget? I've got to help you pick a dress that's suitable for this terribly important party.

NOUR. Do you mind if I go?

AHMAD. I'd say the light-green dress, that floaty, summery, sleeveless one. You like it and it really suits you.

NOUR. You're shouting. I can hear you perfectly well, there's no need to speak so loudly. Do you mind if I go?

AHMAD. Yes I do, actually. I'm shouting because I'm having to compete with the call to prayer, can't you hear it? And yes, I do mind – I want you to let me finish what I'm saying. Or don't you like my taste in clothes?

NOUR. Please, please let me go, I really am tired of this.

AHMAD. I really was going to hit him today, I was that close. It was the first time – well, it wasn't the first time I've thought of doing it, but this time I was actually going to do it.

NOUR. And now you want to hit me… Do you mind if I go? I've got to go.

AHMAD. Maybe it's because I've started counting his observations and comments. He's always been like this. Today he came into the room to wake me up, sometimes I feel like he hates to see me sleeping. My mum says that now he's retired he gets bored all the time and I just have to put up with him. Hasn't she been putting up with him for more than thirty years now? She's developed some sort of immunity.

NOUR. Is there anything you want from me before I go?

AHMAD. He woke me up to tell me for the thousandth time that there's a new job with my brother in Dubai. He knows I hate Dubai and the whole of the Gulf, but obviously it's just because he worries about me, because he's got to think of my future.

NOUR. Look at me for a second.

AHMAD. I wonder how I would've felt if I'd hit him after we argued today. My mum would have cried. Maybe I was too harsh. The truth is that I didn't feel anything inside me… Have I really got cruel?

NOUR. Look at me for a second.

AHMAD. I'm going to go out with my friends. You should sleep more.

NOUR. Ahmad... Ahmad, just for a second.

AHMAD. See you tomorrow.

NOUR. Ahmad...


## Scene Seven

NOUR *puts a large red candle on the table and lights it.*

AHMAD. A new candle?

NOUR. It smells really nice. I hope you don't put it away once I'm gone like you usually do. I thought we could sit by candlelight this time.

*She goes to turn off the light.*

AHMAD. Do you mind if we leave the light on?

NOUR. If you like.

AHMAD. Tomorrow I'm going to give Omar a key to the room.

NOUR. Why?

AHMAD. I don't know. I haven't asked him. He told me he wanted to come with Samar and I told him it was fine.

NOUR. We've only been renting this room for a few days and Omar already wants to bring his girlfriend here. You could at least have asked me. You know I'm not that keen on him.

AHMAD. I don't mind, I've never minded about what you think of people, even though I don't tend to agree with you.

NOUR. You don't pay close attention to him. It's been a long time since I last saw him sober. He's starting to look really unpleasant.

AHMAD. It's true, I don't pay attention, but the fact is it doesn't really matter to me. Anyway, I haven't been seeing him or anyone else much at all recently. Maybe he's happy like that, maybe that's the only way he can be happy. You don't know anything about the situation he's in. At least he's uncomplicated, he's honest.

NOUR. I don't care about his situation, I just care about the fact that he's coming here with his girlfriend. I mean, we don't want problems with the neighbours. Is that your third glass you're on now? Don't you think that's enough? Aren't you meant to be giving up?

AHMAD. You're right... I am cutting back. This'll be my last one.

NOUR. Your fourth? So, you're going to get drunk, are you? And tomorrow we're not going to be able to come here because of that drunk.

AHMAD. He may be a drunk, but at least he's not a lying, arrogant opportunist.

NOUR. I know who you're talking about, but at least those people have jobs. They work hard. They're doing something serious with their lives.

AHMAD. Oh yes, very serious. Being hypocrites and looking good and wearing nice clothes to hide the rottenness and dirt underneath them.

NOUR. That's the simplest excuse you can make for not getting on with my friends. Please stop drinking.

AHMAD. Tomorrow I'll tell Omar to clean himself up and borrow some proper clothes from someone and learn how to be charming and how to lie with every word he speaks. So he can be presentable and so job opportunities will just open up in front of him, opportunities to mix with the hard-working types and join that respectable group of serious people who pass judgement on everyone else.

NOUR. You're drunk.

AHMAD. Not yet...

*He puts out the candle with his hand.*

And they don't stop harping on to each other about how challenging and important their work is and they're disgusted by people who don't do any work and who look horrible and spoil the view and ruin the lovely atmosphere...

NOUR. I think that's enough for today. It's still early and you've almost finished a bottle. Aren't you planning on going home?

AHMAD. Don't be scared, I'm not drunk. Anyway, I've got to finish the story, the story of the future of Omar, the one who's coming. Why don't you have a drink with me? You haven't had a drink for ages.

NOUR. No thank you, I think I'm going to let you finish the evening on your own. Or maybe you could tell the story to Omar.

AHMAD. That's not a bad idea, but stay here with me, maybe you'll change your mind this time.

NOUR. Thank you, but I don't want to.

AHMAD. It's strange how we can love people who are lying to us and cheating us, as long as they do it nicely. Yesterday I saw your old boyfriend, he was very well dressed and he was walking along like he was the king of the world.

NOUR. Why are you bringing this up now? You know I don't like talking about it.

AHMAD. No, no, no, don't worry about it. Trust me, one glass won't do any harm.

NOUR. You're determined to get drunk and I have no desire to be here when you are.

AHMAD. And then I saw a woman I hadn't seen for ages. She's getting on a bit, but she's very pretty. All of us in the neighbourhood were waiting for her to go by, even the women, everybody, that's how amazing she looks. I barely recognised her when I saw her. She really had changed so I asked what had happened and people told me that a year ago she had a serious illness. The amazing thing was that when I saw her she was still walking in the same way. Even though she looks so different, she still holds her head up high, her eyes are still pretty. I stared at her with the same admiration as I always used to and she noticed me out of the corner of her eye just like she always did and ignored me just like she always did. She walked just as proudly and confidently as ever. The grocer I was standing next to sneered and said, 'My heart weeps,' and our neighbour, who was standing with us, just made fun of her misfortune. I wanted to catch up with her and ask her how she was and tell her that I still thought she was really beautiful, but I was scared, like usual, and she disappeared off into the distance with that quick walk of hers, leaving people talking about her just like usual while she walked off without even turning round... Am I a coward?

NOUR. You really have had enough. Stop drinking now.

AHMAD. A coward, I feel so weak and defeated.

NOUR. But you're not.

AHMAD. Maybe that's what it looks like from the outside. You know what?

NOUR. What?

AHMAD. Let's run away.

NOUR. Where to?

AHMAD. I don't know, just away.

NOUR. Okay then.

AHMAD. But first have a drink with me.

**Scene Eight**

AHMAD. Before you got here today the guy who owns the room knocked on the door. I didn't open up but the music was on loud so he must have realised there was someone inside who just didn't want to open the door. Do you think he wanted money?

NOUR. He can't have done, we haven't even been here for twenty days and we agreed we'd pay him on the first of every month. You could've opened the door and found out what he wanted.

AHMAD. I could have… It's very hot, isn't it? Even without my shirt on.

NOUR. You know you've got a really good body. I really love it. Let's not let this hot weather put us off.

AHMAD. I've just had a shower. I really think I should finish the article now, it's already late.

NOUR. You still don't want me… Are you really not attracted to me?

AHMAD. You've got to let me know what you really think about the article.

NOUR. Don't you want me?

AHMAD. I'm scared.

NOUR. Of me… I don't want you to worry about anything.

AHMAD. Of you and of myself and of everything, and I'm scared for you too.

NOUR. I can stop you being scared, but you clearly don't want me.

AHMAD. I can't tell you how much I want you, but let's just wait a bit. Trust me, it'll be better that way.

NOUR. I'm going to take a shower... What do you think, why don't we have a shower together?

AHMAD. No, I've just had a shower, but can you leave the door open?

NOUR. No, I don't want to.

AHMAD. Just a bit, so I can carry on talking to you.

NOUR. Okay.

*She goes into the bathroom, and until the end of the scene we can only hear her voice while she showers.*

AHMAD. Have you ever been with anyone in the shower before?

*Pause.*

Okay. I'm sorry.

NOUR. No, don't worry. Yes, I have.

AHMAD. Who?

NOUR. It doesn't matter... More than one person. People I used to love, or used to think I loved.

AHMAD. Is there anything we can do together for the first time?

NOUR. Everything... Everything feels new with you, with new love.

AHMAD. I'm not talking about how it feels, I'm talking about something that's actually new.

NOUR. I don't know... Seriously, when I think about my previous relationships, there are a lot of things I can't explain. Relationships I really don't know why I got involved in. Maybe I've got a problem... Some sort of uncontrollable need for someone else in my life, or maybe it's something to do with my mum acting as if it was her who was in those relationships, as if through them she could have the youth she missed out on when she was my age.

AHMAD. And maybe I'm just another object of this uncontrollable need of yours… Nour, are you crying? Nour…

NOUR. Yes.

AHMAD. It doesn't matter.

## Scene Nine

NOUR. Where were you today? I kept on trying to call you, why didn't you pick up?

AHMAD. I was filling out some forms.

NOUR. What forms? Why didn't you tell me about them before?

AHMAD. They're not important. Passport application forms.

NOUR. Why now? Has something changed?

AHMAD. Not exactly, it's strange, though, I seem to be getting a bit more practical and thinking about my options.

NOUR. You mean going away; but you've told me so many times that there's no way you'd leave here.

AHMAD. I'm not going to go tomorrow or anything, but the idea doesn't seem so completely out of the question any more. Today when I went into town early – it was the first time I'd done that in ages – it felt so hot and crowded, and then there are all those administrative offices I had to go to, and you know how I've got a real phobia of them.

NOUR. Talking of the overcrowding and the traffic, today they told us that they might give us a car for our department – that means a car for three employees. Obviously, we'd use it for all our work trips, but we could share it between us when we're not using it for work too. What do you think about that? I need to get a driving licence as soon as possible.

AHMAD. Great… But the problem today wasn't really the
traffic, the problem was that I was scared of people all the
time. I mean, not scared of one particular person, I just felt
like I wanted to run away from them all the time. When I
decided to go to a café in the old town I couldn't manage to
sit there for more than a quarter of an hour before I felt like I
wanted to run away again. It was so crowded there too…
When I left the al-Hamidiyeh souk I couldn't find any sort of
transport and there was a moment when I felt like I was being
strangled… Seriously, people were coming and going,
everyone was in a rush and I was sure no one knew why. I
started feeling dizzy, it looked like the faces of the people
around me were repeating themselves, it looked like everyone
in the crowd had the same face, and they were all hurrying
along staring at the ground. There was one very old lady who
noticed me, she wanted to know what was wrong or something, she asked me if everything was all right. By that point I
was sitting on the edge of the pavement, just trying to
breathe. Then, even though I couldn't see very clearly, I
walked off. I carried on walking for more than an hour in the
sun until I got here. Maybe I shouldn't go outside again in the
daytime. By the end of the night people have usually settled
down at home and I can walk around more easily.

NOUR. Why have you got so oversensitive to people? You're
running away from everyone, even your friends. You know
one of the things that attracted me to you was that I really
felt you knew how people worked. People liked you, they
were impressed by you.

AHMAD. Maybe… Or maybe even then that wasn't really how
it was.

NOUR. Now I feel like you're running away from everything,
you're distancing yourself from everything… What do you
want from people?

AHMAD. Me! You know what I want? I just want people to
leave me alone. I used to want a lot of things from people,
but now I really don't want anything.

NOUR. You know what… I'm scared of you and I'm scared for you at the same time.

AHMAD. You should be.

NOUR. We've had this room for nearly a month now and I still don't feel like I can understand you any better. You don't let me get any closer to you. All we do is think about the past and dig up old memories and I really am getting tired of it. I constantly feel like I should be apologising to you for everything I did before I knew you, but what should I do now? Please tell me.

AHMAD. Nothing… You don't have to do anything. I'm the problem, it's me.

NOUR. Can I hug you?

AHMAD. Of course…

*She hugs him tightly.*

NOUR. Trust me, I love you.

AHMAD. I really do want to.

**Scene Ten**

AHMAD. When did you find time to clean the room?

NOUR. I left work early today because there was a parade.

AHMAD. Oh, I see, so you ran off from the voluntary national parade.

NOUR. Don't tease. I had to come and clean because you, my dear, who should care more because you spend more time here than I do, let the room turn into a tip. And will you kindly tell me why you took down all the pictures? And why there are still things that you haven't taken out of the boxes?

AHMAD. Leave them for a bit, we might not need to take them out at all.

NOUR. What do you mean? That reminds me – we need to pay our rent to the landlord because the first month's over.

AHMAD. You remind me of my mum, dressed like that and doing the cleaning.

NOUR. I can't believe a month's gone by! Can you? Maybe it's because I haven't seen you properly. There we were, thinking that having this room would let us see more of each other. The problem is if I go away for a long time I can't explain it to my family. Even you're not spending much time here any more.

AHMAD. Speaking of my mum, today we actually sat down and talked to each other. I honestly can't remember the last time we talked properly like that. She talked to me about going away to join my brothers. She said my dad won't ever bother me about it again, but she still begged me to think it over.

NOUR. You'll never go away. You don't want to go away; I know what you're like. Why don't you come and give me a hand? I'd rather you didn't just stare at me like that.

AHMAD. No, let me stare, it's better like this… Anyway, you've done enough cleaning for now. I've got a feeling next month's going to be full of parades so you'll be able to come here as early as you like and clean to your heart's content.

NOUR. Stop staring at me, you're making me laugh. Honestly, that's enough.

AHMAD. I'm thinking about doing what my mum says. Seems to me it's the only solution.

NOUR. Am I really looking that much prettier today?

AHMAD. My mum has strange powers of persuasion.

NOUR. Okay, I'll always wear this dressing gown. Maybe you'll want me more like this. Come on then, why don't you give in to me right now without even thinking about it?

AHMAD. What does being away from home really mean, anyway? I can't understand anything any more; I mean, am I not alienated here? Am I not away here?

NOUR. Now…?

AHMAD. When can we spend a whole night together?

NOUR. I don't know… It's just that I don't know what to say to my family. But I've got to do it at some point.

AHMAD. Don't worry about it, we can wait a few more days, things will be clearer soon. Just stay calm about it for now.

NOUR. You want to leave me… I know you do, I can feel it.

AHMAD. Leave you? You won't believe me when I say this, but it'd be better for you like that… You know something, sometimes I feel like you're a small child and I get so scared for you.

NOUR. Do you really believe it'd be good for me if you left me?

AHMAD. So, so scared.

### Scene Eleven

NOUR. The noise outside is unbearable.

AHMAD. Why don't we ask them to keep it down a bit? You know, ask them to celebrate a bit more quietly.

NOUR. Very funny… Why don't we get out of here and go for a walk? I've still got a couple of hours till I have to be back at home.

AHMAD. Where could we go with the city in this state? No, I'd prefer to stay locked up in here.

NOUR. My mum was saying it's never been like this before.

AHMAD. Maybe… We'll have to wait and see, no one really knows.

NOUR. So, you don't want to go out?

AHMAD. We can't go out now, though I am thinking about going out, going away.

NOUR. I've got an idea, why don't we go up Mount Qasioun? At least it's cool up there and the air's cleaner.

AHMAD. I feel sorry for Qasioun. It's meant to be a huge mountain but it's started to look more like the seaside – kiosks and people competing to sell cigarettes and tea and coffee and music, crowds of people who go up there to eat corn on the cob and seeds. Every time they go up they look out over Damascus beneath them with the same amazement, and it's the same Damascus that they choke and they're choked by all the rest of the time, the same place that they spoil and cover with dirt. At night, once the trampling of people's legs over it eases and the black smog lifts and it starts to be able to breathe and heal its wounds and hide its flaws, people go out onto Qasioun to eat corn on the cob and seeds and look out lovingly and romantically at the view they have from above.

NOUR. That'll do... I don't want to go out any more. You've got very tense.

AHMAD. I've been trying for so long but I haven't been able to write a single word, not a single letter.

NOUR. You've been like that for a while... And now you've missed your deadlines and you've got some apologising to do.

AHMAD. I don't know what's happening to me, even when I'm alone in the room here. I thought it was just that I needed a place where I could be on my own.

NOUR. Maybe it's because of the noise, maybe it's because you don't really like the room. I don't mind if you want to stay at home more.

AHMAD. This morning I decided to stay at home for a bit and I realised my dad was desperate for an excuse to talk to me. He talked to me about an old article of mine that he read and made a few comments about it. When he saw me carrying on working without responding to what he said, he went away quietly. I could see him perfectly well without having to turn round to look at him. I pitied him for the first time, then. I realised I'd never like to be in his position.

NOUR. What position's that?

AHMAD. When I was little, I used to stare at the shelves full of old books that he'd kept since he was a young man. It was him who encouraged me to read, but something changed – maybe he couldn't stand up to the pressures of life any more, or maybe he never really cared about things like that, or maybe he, like so many people, just ended up following the herd. In the end, the cultured man he had been gave up and life and its routine wore him down until he turned into nothing more than a dim-witted teacher who couldn't forget, not even for a single second, that he had to be a father to us, but in the worst sort of way.

NOUR. Sometimes I'm afraid that we all repeat our parents' mistakes. Do you think maybe that's just natural?

AHMAD. I think maybe I can't stay here any longer.

NOUR. I don't understand you.

AHMAD. Don't worry about it. I can't even understand myself. I think we should spend the night together here next week. What do you think? Do you think we can?

NOUR. I'll tell my family I'm going to stay the night at my friend Leila's.

AHMAD. Look at me closely...

NOUR. What?

AHMAD. I'm sorry.

NOUR. For what?

AHMAD. For everything.

**Scene Twelve**

AHMAD. Forget about the music, there's no time.

NOUR. Did you choose tonight as our night together on purpose?

AHMAD. I could only do it tonight… I wanted it to be this particular night. I've been looking forward to it for so long.

NOUR. I told you I knew you were going to leave me. You can go, I don't want you any more.

AHMAD. Maybe I was never really with you. Maybe I couldn't have been with anyone.

NOUR. It's actually my fault – I should have known, all the clues were there.

AHMAD. I've been looking forward to this night for so long. I wanted it to be just one nice memory of this whole place to make me feel more attached to it, but it looks like all I've done is hurt you… Now there's nothing that can make me feel attached to this town. I'm suffocating here and you, more than anyone, could see that just now.

NOUR. You really can go now, before all the nice memories that I have of this room disappear.

AHMAD. Okay then, can we just listen to that music we like one last time?

*Pause.*

I didn't want things to be like this. There are a lot of things that I don't understand but one thing I'm sure of is that I'll always remember you… Goodbye.

*A knock on the door.*

NOUR. Do you want to listen to the music?

AHMAD. Just for five minutes.

NOUR. That's enough.

AHMAD. Are you going to cry?

NOUR. I'll try to stop myself.

AHMAD. I won't be able to.

NOUR. You can cry, it won't make me angry. Just let me hug you.

AHMAD. I'm really scared.

NOUR. Me too.

AHMAD. Will you be all right when I'm gone?

NOUR. It doesn't matter. You?

AHMAD. I don't know… I don't know anything.

*More knocking on the door.*

NOUR. It's time.

AHMAD. No, we've still got five minutes.

*The End.*

**603**

IMAD FARAJIN

*translated by*

HASSAN ABDULRAZZAK

**Imad Farajin**

Imad Farajin has worked as an actor for nine years and started writing plays in 2002. He studied acting at the Liverpool Institute of Performing Arts. He performed in Al-Kasaba Theatre's *Alive from Palestine: Stories Under Occupatio*n, which was devised by the company and has toured throughout the world. In 2007 he won the Al-Qattan Foundation's Young Writer Award for his play *Chaos*. Imad also writes extensively for television.

**Hassan Abdulrazzak**

Hassan Abdulrazzak is of Iraqi origin, born in Prague and living in London. His first play, *Baghdad Wedding*, was staged at Soho Theatre, London, in 2007 and Belvoir St Theatre, Sydney, in 2009. It was also broadcast on BBC Radio 3 in 2008. Hassan was awarded the 2008 George Devine and Meyer-Whitworth Awards and the 2009 Pearson Award. He has been published in the *Guardian*, *Edinburgh Review*, *Banipal* and *Snakeskin*.

*603* was first performed as a rehearsed reading as part of the *I Come From There: New Plays from the Arab World* season in the Jerwood Theatre Upstairs, Royal Court Theatre, London, on 14 November 2008, with the following cast:

| | |
|---|---|
| MOSQUITO | Lee Ross |
| BOXMAN | Nathaniel Martello-White |
| SLAP | Tom Fisher |
| SNAKE | Matt Smith |
| SIREN | Houda Echouafni |
| *Director* | Rufus Norris |

The play was also read at Al Balad Theatre in Amman, Jordan, in February 2009. A production of *603*, directed by Manal Awad, toured various theatres in the West Bank, Palestine, and Dubai and Abu Dhabi.

## Characters

MOSQUITO
BOXMAN
SLAP
SNAKE

SIREN, *a girl in her mid-twenties*

## Setting

Askalan Central Prison, a prison cell with four beds and a side bathroom.

## Notes and references

*Haja* – a lady who has been to the annual pilgrimage in Mecca
*Hayal* – a soldier (Hebrew)
*Shotair* – a guard (Hebrew)

The literal translation of the song Snake sings on pages 39 and 60 is 'The bride descended to the circle of the groom. Glory to Mohammed, shame to Satan.'

*The light goes up gradually. Everyone is sleeping except*
MOSQUITO *who is holding a plastic cup. He is tapping on it a*
*variety of rhythms, quietly. He has an empty matchbox open on*
*the floor. He is scanning the room for a mosquito. He looks up*
*towards the ceiling. A mosquito appears and flies into the open*
*matchbox.* MOSQUITO *closes the box and goes back to bed.*

BOXMAN *takes out a plastic cup from his box. He places it on*
*the floor and then puts his ear to the cup to listen through it,*
*before moving somewhere else.*

BOXMAN. The buses are here, the buses are here, on my
    mum's honour, the buses are here.

   MOSQUITO *and* SLAP *wake up.* SNAKE *carries on*
   *sleeping.*

   Come here. Listen to the sound of the buses. These are the
   buses coming to take us. (*He dances.*) That's it, boys. It looks
   like they're about to exchange us for Gilad Shalit, the Israeli
   soldier. Come here, listen. We're leaving, we're going home.
   The letter was true. We're going to be released this week.

   MOSQUITO *and* SLAP *go to listen.* MOSQUITO *puts his*
   *ear to the cup.*

MOSQUITO. God, it does sound like buses!

SLAP. Let me listen… I think it's the sound of buses.

BOXMAN. Man, it's the sound of buses.

MOSQUITO. It's clear now, one hundred per cent, it's the
    sound of buses.

SLAP. Brothers, clearly and surely it's the sound of buses.

MOSQUITO. I want to say this to you, it is definitely the sound
    of buses, the sound of buses arriving… but I also hear women.

BOXMAN. What?

MOSQUITO. Women laughing.

BOXMAN. Maybe they're the drivers.

MOSQUITO. I tell you women, you tell me drivers!

BOXMAN. Women could be drivers, man. The world has changed. Your mind is still set to nine years ago; today everything is different.

MOSQUITO. You really think they'd use women drivers to transport inmates who've spent at least eight years inside? There're guys in here that could impregnate a rock.

BOXMAN. Man, you're so removed from reality. Give it here, I want to listen.

SLAP *coughs*.

I can't hear over your coughing, Slap… wait, I can hear the flashes of cameras making a 'tcheeck tcheeck' sound.

MOSQUITO. That's not right. Camera flash is 'tcheck tchook, tcheck tchook'.

BOXMAN. Man, that was nine years ago. Nowadays cameras make a 'tcheeck tcheeck' sound.

MOSQUITO. Bullshit, let me listen. (*Puts his ear to the cup.*) There, 'tcheeck tchook, tcheeck tchook'.

SLAP. May I? To be honest I can't hear neither 'tcheeck tcheeck' or 'tcheeck tchook'… I hear 'tcheeck tchack… tcheeck tchack'… But there are people speaking in English.

BOXMAN. They must be working for the Red Cross. That's it. Tonight the exchange is going to happen. They're here to supervise the exchange, the give and take. Slap, let Mosquito listen. He speaks good English. His wife was Canadian.

MOSQUITO. And a bitch. Give it here. What's this? Someone is saying to a girl 'Give me a kiss.'

BOXMAN. What does it mean?

MOSQUITO. It means give me a kiss.

BOXMAN. Maybe it's Shalit? It's been a long time since he's seen his sister. He's asking her to give him a kiss. What's wrong with a man kissing his sister?

MOSQUITO. God give me patience… What a donkey you are.

SLAP. English is not my strongest language but I think 'kiss' is used in a girlfriend-boyfriend situation, whereas 'French kiss' is used amongst family.

BOXMAN. Now you're both experts on kissing!

MOSQUITO. Shh… I can hear the clanking of keys.

*Silence. They look at one another.*

SLAP. It's happening tonight.

BOXMAN. Tonight?

MOSQUITO. Tonight.

MOSQUITO *opens the matchbox and looks at the mosquito inside. He then looks at* SNAKE *who is still sleeping. He goes towards his bed.*

I wish tonight never came.

BOXMAN (*angrily*). What? You wish it never came?! I wish it came years ago. What are you saying? Are you mad? You don't want to go, then don't. Me, I'm going. I want to see Siren. Eight years, I've been waiting. And you say, 'I wish tonight never came.' Siren's hair must've turned grey with waiting by now. I want to take her and fly. I want to see life. I love life. Why the fuck did I throw that petrol bomb?

MOSQUITO. And what about Snake?!

*Silence.*

BOXMAN. What about Snake?

MOSQUITO. We leave him here, all alone?

BOXMAN (*in a low voice*). What do you want us to do? He's
serving twelve life sentences. The man is never getting out of
here. Look, if my dear old dad himself was serving life here,
I'd still leave him behind. We don't want to be tied to him.
Let's just get out of this place and forget all about it.

SNAKE (*from under the covers*). Like Mosquito says, I'm here
for life. No blue skies for me. (*To* MOSQUITO.) Go, find
your daughter; she must be a grown woman by now. I'll be
here. Twelve life sentences mean twelve generations.

*He pulls the cover away, looks at them all.*

Come on, brothers, get ready. Don't just stand there! Move
it, Mosquito. You too, Boxman. Hey, Slap, go on, get going.
What's wrong with you? Come on, what the fuck, guys?
Don't worry about me. Prison is for real men. Anyway,
you'll visit, right? Boxman, you'll come and invite me to
your wedding with Siren. Slap, you've got to have that operation. Come on, brothers, celebrate your freedom!

SNAKE *hands each man his luggage. They hold the luggage
but do not move.*

No goodbyes. I don't like them. Come on, if you love me,
just go…

*He stands aside.*

MOSQUITO. I just want –

SNAKE. Not another word. Goodbye.

SLAP. I…

SNAKE. Look after yourself.

BOXMAN *runs up to* SNAKE *and hugs him.*

Boxman, I want you to love Siren. Love her every day, more
and more. Tickle her!

MOSQUITO, SNAKE *and* SLAP *line up and walk in procession. We hear the sound of the metal door opening. They
dart a glance towards* SNAKE *before exiting.*

SNAKE *gets up and looks towards where they went. He then takes the plastic cup and places it on the floor, listening to what's going on outside. He begins to sing.*

Here comes the bride, dancing for her groom,
Kicking the devil way beyond the moon.

*At the same time, we hear* SIREN *breathing as she runs across the cell.* SNAKE *jumps on the bed and scans all corners of the cell.* SIREN *begins dancing across the cell in search of* BOXMAN. SNAKE *keeps trying to touch her but she escapes. As this is happening,* MOSQUITO *enters slowly, followed by* SLAP.

MOSQUITO *and* SLAP *begin talking with* SNAKE.

MOSQUITO. Outside the world is green… green. Even though it's night-time, I could see the green.

SLAP. The bus door opened and shut.

MOSQUITO. The smell of almond blossom! God, I've forgotten what almonds taste like.

SLAP. And the bus door opened and shut.

MOSQUITO. The air had a touch of cold… but it was a gentle touch.

SLAP. And the bus door opened and shut.

MOSQUITO. The mosquito shivered inside her matchbox.

SLAP. And the bus door opened and shut.

MOSQUITO. I thought she was hungry, turns out she's cold.

SLAP. …Opened and shut.

MOSQUITO. A puppy yapped in the distance.

SLAP. …Opened and shut.

MOSQUITO. And Boxman was puffing away as if he was a nympho and the cigarettes were cocks.

*A sigh of longing is heard from* SIREN.

SLAP. ....Opened and shut...

MOSQUITO. Boxman never smoked before... I looked left and right for my daughter, couldn't see her.

SLAP. And the bus door opened and shut... and the pup barked from far away.

MOSQUITO. And the bus door shut and didn't open... It turns out today is their Independence Day. They've come to celebrate. And they wanted us to fetch wood for them. So they could start a fire and dance around it.

SLAP. I wish I could've seen that fire lit and danced around it also, but Mosquito refused to collect the wood so we were sent back.

MOSQUITO. Man, you can't even dance! You barely know how to walk.

SLAP. When Slap went to weddings, he'd wear a pink suit and put a flower in the breast pocket. I'd dance from the beginning till the end of the wedding. People thought I must be the groom because I was always so happy.

*We hear* BOXMAN *outside*. SIREN *leaves*.

BOXMAN. Open the door, why've you closed it? Hey, *shotair... hayal...* Open the door. Fine, no problem, I can wait outside till morning. You son of a dog, don't pretend you can't hear me. I'll get you, you Ethiopian bastard. Or is the brother from Morocco? Better go and find out who your father is, could be Indian for all you know. Mosquito, man... come and help me out, I'm rubbish at Hebrew. You could talk to them in English... Tell them, no need for the buses to go... there're only two hours left till morning. Tomorrow, they could take me to Gaza... and later come back to take you to the West Bank. They should sleep a little, otherwise tomorrow they'll turn up drowsy and instead of taking me to Gaza, I'll end up in Guantanamo. Get up, man. No? Fine. I just want to say, I've gone back to smoking and I'll be smoking hash this time and if I can't get hash I'll roll up tea leaves and pretend I'm getting high.

SLAP. Tomorrow comes to those who wait.

BOXMAN. Way I see it, those who wait never see tomorrow.

MOSQUITO *opens the matchbox and observes the mosquito flying out.*

SLAP (*takes out a notebook and begins writing*). 25th April, one o'clock at night. We heard the sound of buses. Mosquito and Boxman began to argue over camera flashes. Mosquito said they made a 'tcheeck tchoock' sound and Boxman said it was 'tcheeck tcheeck'. I didn't want to interfere but the boys were begging me to tell them what I thought. I refused, they begged even more. In prison, my word counts.

I screamed at Mosquito and Boxman. 'Enough,' I said. And I slapped Mosquito so hard, sparks flew out of his eyes. Boxman fled like a cat and hid under the bed.

*Pause.*

I stared at Snake then told him we're leaving. The time for prisoner exchange has come. Mosquito started crying because Snake was going to be left all alone. So I slapped him again. 'Prison is for men,' I said. Then I slapped Snake as he began to cry also. I shouldn't have lost control like that, not in front of the guys, they look up to me. I am the manliest amongst them. Outside we found the buses waiting. The warden's eyes were on me like a hawk's. He knows how tough I am. Everyone knows the story of Slap, the secondary-school teacher who slapped the soldier when he dared to touch one of his pupils. I slapped him, once, twice, three times… I slapped him till he lost consciousness… His buddy leapt on me and slammed down the butt of his rifle on my head. He hit me so hard, I slapped him back and I slapped him and slapped him… I want to slap and slap…

SLAP *completely loses control over his mind and body. SNAKE goes up to him and carries him to bed. He gives him a tranquilliser pill.* MOSQUITO *and* BOXMAN *have a conversation in a low tone.*

MOSQUITO. He's been writing for six years. He used to write one letter a month, now it's one per day. I feel he's mocking us. He's the only one that doesn't talk about his private life.

BOXMAN. Man, he must have close to a thousand letters hidden.

MOSQUITO. Where?

BOXMAN. Under his bed; I saw him one night sorting them out, dozens and dozens.

MOSQUITO. Slap is a devious bastard. He's like the water of a river. On the surface, nothing but calm, but underneath the current runs and runs… He hates my mosquito, every time I want to feed her, he starts causing trouble. Marxists are like that, love no one but themselves.

BOXMAN. You know, sometimes I feel he's a good man. Hey, look, what's with Snake lately, always going to the toilet… back and forth… spends the whole night there.

MOSQUITO. Could be constipated… too embarrassed to talk about it.

BOXMAN. Come on, Snake embarrassed? Since when?

MOSQUITO. Sometimes I envy him.

BOXMAN. Envy him what?

MOSQUITO. He's not waiting for anything. He knows he'll be spending the rest of his life in prison.

BOXMAN. If I had to spend the rest of my life here, I'd kill myself. You know what I think? The minute we leave here, he's going to hang himself.

MOSQUITO. Snake wouldn't do that.

BOXMAN. You give him too much credit, man.

SNAKE (*from the bathroom*). What's up, Boxman?

BOXMAN. Everything's cool, bro. (*To* MOSQUITO.) What we said stays between us.

MOSQUITO. Don't worry, if there's one thing I hate in life, it's betrayal.

BOXMAN. Because of your wife.

MOSQUITO. I don't want to think about her.

BOXMAN. Man, if you stood up for the judge, you wouldn't be here, waiting for the prisoner exchange. You'd be outside, waiting to greet us when we come out.

MOSQUITO. I don't care if I have to rot in here for a hundred years, I would never stand up for that judge. They occupy us and then dare to judge us? Are you crazy? I'll never do it.

BOXMAN. You could've done it for the sake of your daughter.

MOSQUITO. What daughter, man? I have no idea where her bitch of a mother has taken her.

BOXMAN. Take it easy.

MOSQUITO. No, I won't. And I'll never stand for no judge even if I have to endure a life sentence like Snake.

SNAKE. Everything all right, Mosquito?

MOSQUITO *is silent.*

BOXMAN. So, if they tell you, 'Unless you stand up for the judge, you won't be going home tonight,' what would you do?

SLAP. We all exaggerate.

MOSQUITO. How's it going, Slap?

SLAP. Just dandy.

MOSQUITO. Come on, boys, before you go to bed, let's feed the mosquito. She looks hungry.

BOXMAN. Man, you haven't fed her yet? It's two in the morning. How could you?

MOSQUITO. Give me your finger, not the one you put out at lunch, another.

BOXMAN. I can't remember which finger I gave you at lunch.

MOSQUITO. The middle.

BOXMAN. Fine, take the index.

MOSQUITO. Has she bitten you?

BOXMAN. Not yet.

MOSQUITO. Now?

BOXMAN. Not yet.

MOSQUITO. Now?

BOXMAN. Not yet.

MOSQUITO. Change fingers.

BOXMAN. Why?

MOSQUITO. You've put her off; God knows where you've stuck it.

BOXMAN. What? She could smell?

MOSQUITO. Of course. So where have you been putting it?

BOXMAN. Nowhere.

MOSQUITO. Liar. I'm going to ask her. (*Takes the matchbox to one side and asks the mosquito inside.*) What? Ha ha ha. Really…? Ha ha ha –

BOXMAN. What's she saying?

MOSQUITO. Shame on you. Give me another.

BOXMAN *puts out another finger.*

Has she bitten you?

BOXMAN. Not… Ouch. She bit me!

MOSQUITO. Thanks… (*Goes to* SLAP.) Please give me your hand and be quick about it.

SLAP. Piss off, you and your mosquito! I'll slap you and slap her.

MOSQUITO. Put your hand out, man, and let this poor creature have her supper.

*He grabs one of* SLAP's *fingers and puts it inside the matchbox.*

Did she bite you?

SLAP. No.

MOSQUITO. What about now?

SLAP. Ouch. This is the last time I'm feeding her.

MOSQUITO (*goes to* SNAKE). Give me yours… She bit you?

SNAKE. She bit me.

MOSQUITO (*to* SNAKE). You never say 'ouch'. (*To the mosquito.*) Satisfied? You want pudding? I don't think so, you've put on weight. Don't be like that, it's an honest observation. Look how your arse wobbles. All you mosquitoes are the same, if someone tries to tell you the truth, you get upset. Tell me, do you think Sama, my daughter, has heard about the prisoner exchange? Maybe she's waiting outside for me. But even if she is, how will I know it's her? I've never seen her in my life.

SLAP. For years, you've been telling the mosquito the same story. 'You want pudding?'; 'You've put on weight'; 'How your arse wobbles.' Find something new to talk about with her.

MOSQUITO. Something has changed. I dreamt last night she was sleeping on the bed, turning left and right, then she fell off the bed. When I picked her up, she was dead.

SLAP. It was a nightmare.

SNAKE *is listening all this time.* MOSQUITO *closes the matchbox.* SNAKE *goes to* MOSQUITO.

SNAKE. Mosquito.

MOSQUITO. Yes.

SNAKE. You…

MOSQUITO. What about me?

SNAKE *wants to say something but then changes his mind.*

SNAKE. You miss your daughter?

MOSQUITO. Very much.

SNAKE. So, when a man marries and has children… he gets closer.

MOSQUITO. Closer to what?

SNAKE. To his parents.

MOSQUITO. Sounds like you're ready to be a dad.

SNAKE. No, not at all… it's nothing… I was just asking.

SLAP. When a man gets older, he starts to think about these things… settling down… without even thinking, his emotions just carry him forward.

SNAKE. My emotions are dead, Slap. I don't let myself think about these things. I know where my path is taking me… Give us a cig, Mosquito. (*He lights it.*) I need to take a crap… Guys, do you want to use the toilet before I go in there? I'm staying all night. Boxman, how about you?

BOXMAN. You go and enjoy yourself. I'm waiting for the bus. No time to sleep.

SNAKE. Ah, you want to wait for the bus.

SNAKE *takes the cigarette with him to the bathroom. The rest sleep, with the exception of* BOXMAN. BOXMAN *goes to the door and tries to listen with the aid of the plastic cup. Then he goes and sits on his box. Meanwhile,* SNAKE *looks out of the bathroom calmly to see if everyone is asleep. He notices* BOXMAN *and hides quickly.* BOXMAN *walks slowly towards the bathroom and tries to listen to what's going on inside. He puts his ear to the door. Suddenly,* SNAKE *reaches out and grabs him by the neck.*

BOXMAN. Oh, bollocks!

SNAKE. When I was twelve, I'd spend the day catching young snakes in the valley. I'd stick them in a bucket and head east, towards the settlements. I'd hide behind a boulder and wrap the baby snakes around rocks. And when a bus came, carrying settlers, I'd chuck my snake-load at it. The windows smash. The snakes uncoil and run amok between their legs. I watch the settlers run like crazy inside the bus... Never do that again... I know you fear the Snake.

*A movement intermission.*

*Next day. The light increases. The men walk in one row to the front of the stage.*

MOSQUITO. 2002.

SNAKE. 704.

SLAP. 607.

BOXMAN. 301.

*They go back to their beds in one line. They bend in unison. Turn around on the spot.* BOXMAN *takes out the cup and puts it on the ground.*

Stop, boys, I want to hear.

SNAKE *goes to the toilet.* MOSQUITO *goes to his bed. He releases the mosquito from inside the matchbox and follows her flight path. He then begins to put on the clothes he has set aside for his release, all the while observing the flight of the mosquito.*

MOSQUITO. Can you hear anything?

BOXMAN. No, just Snake taking a dump.

MOSQUITO. Snake, how long you going to take?

SNAKE. I'm nearly done. Just wiping.

MOSQUITO. Hurry up... we want to hear the sound of the buses.

SLAP. What do you think about this shirt, Mosquito? I love pink.

MOSQUITO. Ugly… Isn't that the one you wore in court? When you stood up for that judge?

SLAP. Yes, I save it for important occasions.

MOSQUITO. And you consider standing up for the judge a happy occasion?

SLAP. Yes. Just to feel the cool breeze of the air conditioning in the court. It was relaxing.

BOXMAN. I can't hear anything, just dogs barking.

SLAP. It's too early.

BOXMAN. True, it's early. But don't forget the road from here to Gaza is long, and all the streets of Gaza have armed fighters… We want to get there before the call to evening prayer… I want to see Siren… see her face.

MOSQUITO (*observing the mosquito*). If you get there at night, you'll recognise her by her scent.

BOXMAN. All her life, she wore lovely perfumes.

SNAKE *sighs from the bathroom.*

SLAP. Today's perfumes are different from yesterday's.

SNAKE (*from inside the bathroom*). Even after one hundred years, her scent will be familiar to whoever smelled her first.

BOXMAN. I was sixteen the first time I caught a whiff. You know, Slap… the first time I saw her, I was wearing a red shirt. I had a poem prepared. I looked into her eyes and read it… I was just a boy… Here, listen to the first verse:

This way, this way, kiss.
This way, this way, bite.
This way, this way, frown.
This way, this way, tease.

SNAKE (*from inside the bathroom*). This way, this way… shut it!

BOXMAN. She was astonished. It was the first time she'd heard a poem with an internal rhyme.

SLAP. You call this silliness 'poetry'?

BOXMAN. It came to me on the bog. (*Laughs.*)

SNAKE. That explains it.

*They all laugh.*

BOXMAN. Huh, there's a sound.

*He uses the plastic cup to listen.*

SNAKE *comes out of the bathroom and looks at* BOXMAN.

SNAKE. Boxman, come here, I want a word.

BOXMAN. What? Something happened?

SNAKE. I've a Marlboro ciggie; I've been hiding it for ages.

BOXMAN. Marlboro? Oh, what happy day, come, come, let's smoke it before the bus gets here.

SNAKE. We'll smoke it in a sec. Let's go to the corner so Slap and Mosquito won't see us. They'll want a puff.

BOXMAN. You're right, come on... You know when I said you'll never see the sky again, I didn't mean it... Light it.

SNAKE. Don't worry about it, Boxman.

BOXMAN. Light it... light it.

SNAKE. Missing Siren?

BOXMAN. Of course... Do you need to ask... Light it, light it.

SNAKE. When you saw her, you were wearing a red shirt... but what was she wearing?

BOXMAN. A long skirt... Come on, light it.

SNAKE. Skirt... what colour?

BOXMAN. Black, with burgundy embroidered down the side... Come on... the bus will be here any minute.

SNAKE. And her top… what was it like?

BOXMAN. A flowery shirt… Light it.

SNAKE. Shirt??

> SNAKE *lights the cigarette, takes a drag.* BOXMAN *reaches out to take the cigarette,* SNAKE *doesn't let him.*

> What colour…? For God's sake, focus, Boxman.

> BOXMAN *is silent.* SNAKE *gives him the cigarette.*

BOXMAN. Red.

SNAKE. Black skirt, red shirt. (*Takes back the cigarette.*) Was she wearing lipstick?

> BOXMAN *is silent.* SNAKE *gives him the cigarette.*

BOXMAN. Yes, she had red lipstick on.

SNAKE. And did you touch her with your hands?

BOXMAN. Why you asking…? I touched her plenty… Once I cornered her in the chicken coop.

SNAKE (*giving him the cigarette*). Right, right… Well, go on… what happened in the chicken coop?

> BOXMAN *is smoking.*

> Carry on… What happened in the coop?

BOXMAN. I picked her up and put her on the window sill.

SNAKE. What was she wearing?

BOXMAN. Same skirt and shirt.

SNAKE. Black and red, right… She always wears the same clothes… Go on, what happened next?

BOXMAN. I got closer… and then I cornered her.

SNAKE (*takes back the cigarette*). Wow! Your legs between hers?

> BOXMAN *nods.*

Go on, go on.

BOXMAN. Yes. I cornered her, and then…

SNAKE. Go on, don't stop, what happened next?

BOXMAN. She looked at me and closed her eyes.

SNAKE (*takes back the cigarette*). She was enjoying it… Well, don't stop.

BOXMAN. I put my hand…

SNAKE. Where? Where did you put your hand?

BOXMAN (*realising the cigarette is finished*). I can hear something… Sounds like the bus is here.

BOXMAN *goes*.

SNAKE. Finish it, for fuck's sake. Finish it. Fuck the bus. Finish it.

BOXMAN *takes out the plastic cup and begins to listen*.

BOXMAN. Huh, there's a sound.

The buses are here. The buses are here. I want to get to Gaza before dark.

MOSQUITO *takes out a cup, taps on it… The mosquito returns and goes inside the matchbox*.

MOSQUITO. Guys, we've got to feed the mosquito so she doesn't get dizzy on the bus.

BOXMAN. Why would she get dizzy? Is she pregnant or something?

MOSQUITO. Don't be a smart arse… Has she bitten you?

BOXMAN. Not yet.

MOSQUITO. Has she bitten you?

BOXMAN. Not yet.

MOSQUITO. Has she bitten you?

BOXMAN. Not yet.

MOSQUITO. Has she bitten you?

BOXMAN. Ouch! She did.

MOSQUITO. Give me your hand, Slap.

SLAP. Fuck off.

MOSQUITO. Ha ha ha… Come on now… enough with the jokes.

SLAP. Who says I'm joking?

MOSQUITO. We've been feeding her for seven years. You always went along with it.

SLAP. Today I refuse.

MOSQUITO. Don't piss me off.

BOXMAN. For God's sake, the buses are waiting.

SLAP. I don't have enough blood today.

MOSQUITO. Yes you do.

SLAP. I don't.

BOXMAN. For God's sake.

MOSQUITO (*to* SLAP). Give me your hand before I break it.

SLAP. Clear off! Before I slap you and slap who slaps you.

BOXMAN. Snake.

MOSQUITO. Fine, Slap, be like that… I'll sort you out later… This mosquito, which you refuse to feed, pissed off the highest judge in all of Israel, she circled around his head, landing on his nose, then on his ears. She made him so nervous, he had to leave the court, at a time when the gallons of blood spilling on our streets failed to move a single hair on his head. Have you forgotten? This little mosquito has done far more than your dear old friend Marx… the one you write about day and night… about his opinions… and theories on Communism and Socialism. The age of Communism has passed. If your friend, Marx, were living today he'd be writing about this mosquito you hate so much. I know what you've been writing. And I'll sort you out soon. Mark my words.

SLAP. There's no time left for that... The bus is here.

MOSQUITO. Dream on.

SNAKE (*reaches out from under the cover*). Come, Mosquito, let her bite me.

MOSQUITO. Not today.

SNAKE. Why not?

MOSQUITO. Listen, mate, I don't want... I don't want this to be the last bite.

SNAKE. A second ago you said he was dreaming... now you talk about 'last bite'... What's going on, Mosquito?

MOSQUITO (*avoiding the question*). You reckon she'll survive outside?

SNAKE. As long as you breathe, she lives.

MOSQUITO. I'll miss you.

SNAKE. Don't forget to visit *haja* Salma, my dad's aunt.

MOSQUITO. Don't worry about it... I'll be happy to do that for you.

*They go out and come back again.* SNAKE *observes them from the bathroom as if they are somewhere else.*

SNAKE. Who, Mosquito? How you've been...? Slap.

MOSQUITO. Hello, Snake.

SNAKE. Slap?? How're you doing, mate?

SLAP. I had the operation. They put a screw in my head.

SNAKE. Where's Boxman?

MOSQUITO. Boxman is on honeymoon. With Siren, they went to Talousa.

SNAKE. And how is your daughter Sama?

MOSQUITO. Says hello.

*He repeats this several times, they all laugh.*

It turns out these were the buses for the next guard shift.

SLAP. We've been hearing them for years... how could they've slipped our minds?

BOXMAN (*from outside*). The buses are here. Seriously. Come, boys, let's get in line before everyone else comes out.

*They continue laughing and saying goodbye to one another.*

*They exit. SNAKE remains alone. No one returns. He approaches the door then turns his back to it and begins singing hysterically. MOSQUITO and SLAP return. They look at SNAKE. SNAKE laughs.*

(*His voice is far away.*) The buses are here. Come on, boys. This time the buses are here for sure.

*Everyone looks at the door with suspicion.*

Come on, Mosquito, Slap, the guard is calling cell block 603. We're the first to board.

*As they exit, they run into BOXMAN, entering.*

Just kidding...! You're so gullible. (*Laughs hysterically.*) The prison authority must love to needle us... but their sense of humour stinks. (*Lets go of the box.*) Why are they torturing us? What have we done? All I want is to marry Siren, and finish my degree in Agriculture; buy a small tractor with a right wing and a left wing; put a small chair for Siren next to me. She'll be seven months pregnant. On the right wing, I'll have a son and on the left wing, a daughter. And another boy running behind the tractor, he'll be the one we always forget about. 'Dad, stop, take me with you.' Fayrouz will be singing 'Last Days of Winter' on the radio... and Siren will split open tomatoes and pop them in my mouth. 'Eat, they'll strengthen your blood… Damn, we've forgotten about the boy again.'

MOSQUITO *goes to* BOXMAN *and hugs him.*

SNAKE. My Grandpa Salama loved to tell jokes. Married *haja* Nasra… crazy Nasra. In the '67 war she went out and started sprinkling rice on the Israeli tanks, thinking they belonged to the Iraqi army. Sprinkling rice and ululating. One of the soldiers inside the tank pulled back a side hatch and said, 'Shalom, *haja*.' She cried, 'Who the hell are you?' and ran back to Grandpa Salama. 'It looks like the Turks are back, Salama. These soldiers are not with the Iraqi army.' Salama tried to reassure her: 'Don't worry, love; tomorrow the Iraqi army will be here.' So every day, *haja* Nasra waited on the bridge leading to our village. She died waiting on that bridge.

*The others perform mourning rituals for the passing of* haja *Nasra.*

BOXMAN. God have mercy on the soul of your grandma.

SNAKE. Thank you, thank you.

MOSQUITO. My condolences.

SLAP. She lives in you.

*This repeats as if they are at a very grave funeral. Slowly the atmosphere changes and becomes more jubilant until it seems they are celebrating* SNAKE's *wedding.*

SLAP *brings his chair to the edge of the stage.* BOXMAN *takes his box to the door and sits on it.*

16-04-2007. Many things happened in the cell block today. The boys heard the sound of buses in the morning and thought they were coming for their release. Idiots! They were so happy. But I knew they were the buses bringing food. I have the ears of a fox. I didn't want to spoil their fun, especially that fool, Boxman.

MOSQUITO *is trying to hear what* SLAP *is saying.*

We went out then came back. A little while later we heard the buses again. I knew what they were for. I was tired and didn't want to go out and come back again. I told the boys these buses are bringing new prisoners. Boxman said, 'That's not true.' I stood up, gave him a piercing look and shouted, 'You calling me a liar?' Then I went up to him… To be honest I didn't go up to him, he came to me… I grabbed him by the hair and slapped him. He cried like a child. I felt sorry for him and went out of the cell. I asked the *shotairs* to call the warden. The warden came, shaking with fear. I looked at him… then I slapped him. His secretary, Dani, she wanted to intervene but I slapped her too and I slapped the guards and I slapped the warden's daughter, Ya'ael, and his son, David, and I slapped his wife… forgotten her name now… then the unit in charge of putting down prisoner revolt tried to stop me. I slapped the first of them, then the second and I slapped and slapped and slapped and I slapped Snake and *haja* Nasra and the Iraqi army, one by one I slapped them all. They all know my story. I was a teacher and the soldier hit one of my pupils. I grabbed hold of the soldier and I slapped him and slapped him and slapped him. The boy died and I carried on slapping and slapping. (*Loses control completely.*)

SNAKE *goes to* SLAP, *picks him up and puts him on his bed.*

SNAKE. I'm beginning to hate this job. If only I didn't run out of fucking bullets. They dried his brain with the butt of their guns. (*Goes to the bathroom.*) He used to get the fit once a week. Now it's daily. And what's worse, he's only got the one pill left. Slap… slaps… for they are the slappers. I wish I hadn't run out of bullets, Slap.

SNAKE, MOSQUITO *and* BOXMAN *suddenly stop. They look in all directions in unison. They then look just up and down. They hear the sound of the mosquito. It's strong. They move together in unison performing a dance (the dance of search).*

(*In a low voice.*) Can you hear that?

BOXMAN. Where's she?

MOSQUITO. Under our stuff.

*They start moving their clothes and beds slowly. They go through the clothes piece by piece. They look astonished.*

SNAKE. What the fuck? (*Sighing.*) She's naked.

BOXMAN. Who's that with her?

SNAKE. What are they doing?

BOXMAN. Is he biting her?

SNAKE (*sighing*). Oh God.

MOSQUITO. Turn around, turn around. Don't stare at them.

SNAKE. They're doing what Boxman and Siren did in the chicken coop.

BOXMAN. We didn't do anything in the chicken coop.

SNAKE (*looks at* BOXMAN). Oh God.

MOSQUITO. Everyone back to his bed. 'Oh God', 'Oh God'… You all turned religious all of a sudden…

*He brushes off the male mosquito.*

Shoo, shoo, get off her, piss off.

BOXMAN *exits.* SNAKE *goes to the bathroom.*

BOXMAN (*from far away*). Your mosquito's a slut; you've raised her badly.

MOSQUITO (*to the mosquito*). Look what scandal you've made. Didn't I tell you, sweetheart, that we have customs and traditions? First he has to ask for your hand in marriage then you can have your wedding night. I want to give you the best wedding and dance and sing at your wedding. (*Sings a lullaby.*) Why doesn't she have photos? Why can't her mum send me her photos from Canada? Her mum… Probably running around with her boyfriend… or maybe she sends the letters but they take long to get here… I wonder if

Sama knows me… Does her mum talk to her about me? I've even forgotten what her mum looks like… it's been seven years since I've seen her.

SLAP *takes the cup and puts it on the floor.*

SLAP. The buses are here… they're here…

SNAKE. It's true, they're here.

MOSQUITO (*laughing*). Don't be ridiculous. We're going to rot in jail.

SLAP. Get up, Boxman. Don't make me slap you and slap who slaps you. Get up before you end up like the boy who cried wolf.

*They go.* MOSQUITO *and* SNAKE *remain. They look at each other. We hear the iron door opening loudly.* SNAKE *comes close to the edge of the stage. Faint rhythmic sounds can be heard.*

SNAKE. The door has opened. Get up, Mosquito… It's the first time in nine years I've heard the door open. Get up. The day you've been waiting for is here. Get up.

SNAKE *goes to* MOSQUITO. SIREN *appears in the corner. She begins to dance like a Sufi.* SNAKE *carries* MOSQUITO *over his shoulder and heads for the door.*

The door is open… the day you've been waiting for is here. It's here, Mosquito… Go, go home. Me, I'm never getting out of here.

MOSQUITO *escapes, runs to his bed and hides.*

MOSQUITO. My wife is running around with her boyfriend and my daughter is lost.

SNAKE. Forget your wife. What matters is your daughter.

MOSQUITO. I've lost everything.

SNAKE. That's it. That's the heart of the story, it's not about standing up to some judge.

MOSQUITO. It's all about the judge. I refuse to stand up for a symbol of our occupation.

SNAKE. Don't be a prick. This is your chance. The prisoner exchange. Take it.

MOSQUITO. I'm worried about what people might say... They'll mock me because of her.

SNAKE. Because of whom?

MOSQUITO. The Canadian.

SNAKE. Fuck them. She's your wife.

MOSQUITO. Was my wife, though I'm still responsible for her... and now she's got a boyfriend.

SNAKE. What do you care? When you get out, divorce her and take back your daughter.

MOSQUITO. I can't be sure... that she's my daughter. Biologically.

SNAKE. Don't say that, man. Sure she's your daughter. One hundred per cent. Your wife was pregnant when she left to Canada... her stomach out to there... and you had a premonition she was going to give birth to a daughter... That's why you chose the name Sama.

MOSQUITO. What if she told her, 'Your father is dead'? Or that her boyfriend is the true father?

SNAKE. So what? The girl will still look like you.

MOSQUITO. And her mum, my wife?

SNAKE. What about her?

MOSQUITO. Haven't you been listening? She left me for someone else.

SNAKE. Abandon who abandons you, my friend... To hell with her... You just worry about your daughter.

MOSQUITO. And my wife?

SNAKE. Forget her.

MOSQUITO. She's her mum.

SNAKE. She's gone.

MOSQUITO. Her mum.

SNAKE. She fucked you good, what do you want with her?

MOSQUITO. No... I love her.

*He goes to his bed and hides.* SNAKE *goes after him.*

SNAKE. If you loved her, how can you be scared to think about someone else loving her? Stand up. Stand up. You're a father.

In two hours, your house will be full of visitors.

*The rhythmic beat intensifies and so does* SIREN*'s spinning.*

People coming and people going. All sorts of people. There'll be the political and the perverted. The wise and the idiotic; the nervous, the fearful and the confused. The imam and the priest. Those with Hamas and those with Fatah. Communists and capitalists, slapper and slapped. In two hours, your house will be full of people talking rubbish, about a world you don't recognise, a land severed like the cord of an overplayed guitar, about a nation slapped in the face and trodden down in fear. In two hours, you'll have your fill. And whatever they ask you, answer it. The honest man has nothing to fear. Two hours and you'll see, you'll see what can't be seen and hear what can't be heard. Two hours and the house will be full. I want you to stand in front of them, glowing, a man. Your feet planted in soil; head, nailed to the sky. Let them touch you but not possess you. Two hours and the house will be full.

(*Sings*.)
    Here comes the bride, dancing for her groom,
    Kicking the devil way beyond the moon.

*He repeats this three times before collapsing on the bed. The music stops.* SIREN *disappears.* BOXMAN *enters.*

BOXMAN. Fuck it. Slap's gone. Gone home. They shut the door in my face. Told me to piss off. Slap tricked them. They called for someone whose name sounded something like 'jab' or 'crap' . Slap lifted his hand and said, 'That's me.' I thought I'd do the same. I told them, 'My name is Khadir.' They said, 'There's no one with that name in the entire prison.' Then I said, 'Actually, my name is Salem.' They told me Salem died two years ago. Why're there so many buses? Coming and going. Turns out, these are the buses for people who served their sentence.

*He sits and begins driving an imaginary bus.*

SNAKE (*to* BOXMAN). Your driving is brilliant. Just brilliant. Driving a bus is like driving a tractor. Easy. Easy. Slow down. Slow down. Watch out for the cars... Slow... slow... Put it in second gear, now third. Sweet. Go on. Go on. Pull up, pull up. Don't be scared. Pull up... brill.

*SNAKE stands before BOXMAN and indicates that he wants to get on the bus.*

BOXMAN. Where to, bro?

SNAKE. How do I know... Wait... Take me to Haifa.

BOXMAN. Haifa? How would I get there? They say it's far.

SNAKE. I don't know, it's got a bridge. Grandpa Salama used to tell me, if you want to smell the sweetest fragrance, go to Haifa.

BOXMAN. Got any money?

SNAKE. Don't be ridiculous.

BOXMAN. What a shit day this is turning out to be. Get in. Get in.

*MOSQUITO looks at BOXMAN as he drives the imaginary bus. MOSQUITO indicates that he wants a ride.*

Where to?

MOSQUITO. Don't know.

BOXMAN. 'Don't know'? I've worked this route for twenty years and no one has ever said that before. Got any money?

MOSQUITO. Nope.

BOXMAN. You don't know where you're going and you've got no money… What a shit day… Get in, get in.

MOSQUITO (*riding behind him*). Looks like there is a problem at Zoqaq Gate. Take another route.

BOXMAN. That's normal, it's time for the school run.

MOSQUITO. School? What time do schools in Canada finish?

BOXMAN. How would I know? Why you asking?

MOSQUITO. I have a daughter studying there.

BOXMAN. What year?

MOSQUITO. I don't know.

BOXMAN. I swear, you don't even know where on earth the Lord has put you.

SNAKE (*to* MOSQUITO). How's it going? (*To* BOXMAN.) Could you step on it a little, you're driving like a pensioner.

MOSQUITO. Yes, hurry please.

SNAKE. Faster.

BOXMAN. Hang on.

MOSQUITO. Faster, Boxman.

SNAKE. Just fucking step on it, man. Fly, fly and take us with you.

BOXMAN. Hang on tight. I'm going over the other cars.

MOSQUITO. Think the rocket, be the rocket.

SNAKE. Fly and set the exhaust pipe on fire… Take us to Haifa… to Spring Hill, to Zakarya and Gabreen House… Yaffa… Al-Nasra… Akka… and the Lion's Well… the watermill, Golan Heights and Dar Yasin.

SIREN *appears and she walks slowly towards the bus.*

BOXMAN. Shit! I want to fly, not slow down.

MOSQUITO. Fly to Canada.

BOXMAN. I want to go to Gaza.

SNAKE. Fly, let the exhaust cough up black smoke. I want to become a shepherd again, running free in the mountains. Say hello to *haja* Salma.

BOXMAN. We're on fire... Fly, fly... Sama, daughter... how I miss you.

BOXMAN. Siren, I'm coming to you. Hang on, baby.

SNAKE. Two hours and the house will be full, two hours and the house will be full, hurry.

MOSQUITO. Take us back to prison, to prison. Turn around, turn around and go back.

SNAKE. Ignore him, ignore him... Keep going.

MOSQUITO. If you don't stop, I'll throw myself out of the window.

SNAKE. Don't listen to him.

SNAKE *holds* MOSQUITO *to prevent him jumping off the bus and sings.*

SIREN *is suddenly in front of the bus.* BOXMAN *presses the breaks. All three collapse on the floor... Silence.*

BOXMAN *approaches* SIREN. *He tries to tell her everything very quickly.*

BOXMAN. Your hair is longer, eyes bigger, smell... just as I remember, neither thinner nor fatter, as you were... but why the black under your eyes? Why've you stopped combing your hair? I've got so much to tell you... so much... I want to talk and talk... I want to marry you and have twenty kids... I'll work like a donkey... Why the dark under your eyes… is it from waiting? What news of our village on the mountain? Still facing the sea? I want to smell you, lose my soul in yours.

SIREN *turns her back and prepares to exit.*

Wait.

SNAKE (*stands in front of* SIREN). Wait… wait.

SIREN *wants to leave. He grabs her by her clothes.*

You've been on my mind for years… I was lost in your smell… your name… talk of you… I imagine your hair, long, braided, straight, kinked, wet, liberated and covered up.

*She tries to leave… He rips her clothes.*

I imagine you sleeping, standing, bent over, waiting for the day to end and night to begin.

BOXMAN *tries to intervene.* SNAKE *pushes him violently out of the way.*

I pull you and you pull back… bite you and you bite back… Stay.

SIREN *tries to leave.* SNAKE *lifts her off the ground. She manages to free herself.*

Call me scum, lowlife, lecherous, treacherous, whatever else you like, but know this… I want you, desire you, dream of you every night, perverse images come and go. I lose myself to them.

SIREN *escapes.*

BOXMAN. Shut up, shut up, shut up… Are you crazy? Fuck you and fuck your father and his father also… you fucking shepherd. What? You've been fantasising about her… she's mine.

SNAKE. Was yours.

*Silence… We hear the metal door shut.*

BOXMAN. You're so selfish… You did this because you knew I am leaving this place and you're stuck here. We're all going except you. I'm going and you'll stay in the darkness and the dampness and the isolation, dying slowly. I'll get married and have kids and whoever said prison is for men is a cunt… and a liar. Prison is the end of men. You're going to die, Snake. Know how? Inside the toilet where you spend all your time… you're going to hang yourself. You pretend to be tough but you're weaker than Mosquito's mosquito… Get ready for death, Snake… because after you see us go, you'll feel as if a knife went through your back and came out of your belly. Your death should be slow, bloodless… You know where they'll bury you? Near Askalan, in the prisoners' graveyard with just a number to mark your grave because all you are is a number… You'll live and die without making a woman pregnant, without leaving behind a son to carry your name… Think about what I'm saying… no woman pregnant… no son to carry your name… Let your death be bloodless, Snake. Let it be a hanging.

SNAKE. Do you want to know what happened to Siren?

BOXMAN. Snake.

SNAKE. She died during the shelling of Gaza.

BOXMAN *goes back to his place… puts his cardboard box down and drives the bus slowly.* MOSQUITO *starts tapping on the plastic cup for the mosquito to return… She doesn't. His tapping intensifies throughout the scene.*

(*To* MOSQUITO.) Your mosquito will come back, don't worry.

MOSQUITO. So says the famous sniper… You're only someone on the outside.

SNAKE. I don't care how people rate me. What matters is what you think.

MOSQUITO. They tell your stories to children before they go to sleep.

SNAKE. I don't care about that, tell me what you think.

MOSQUITO. They tell them about the shepherd who, whenever he stopped, his flock stopped along with him… and when he walked, they walked behind him… Once upon a time, there was a shepherd, holding an old English rifle from the time of Jordan.

SNAKE. Worn out with rust.

MOSQUITO. He roamed the valleys… watching the blockades between the mountains. You fell in love with the love of your friend… lost yourself in a fantasy that didn't belong to you.

MOSQUITO *slaps* SNAKE.

SNAKE. If someone else did that, I'd cut off his hand. What do you want me to do? Outside, they think of me as hero. But what kind of hero am I when I'm rotting here and no one gives a fuck? First two years passed and no one came to visit, yet outside they call me the sniper hero and talk endlessly about how I shot twelve soldiers with a rusty English rifle. Only *haja* Salma comes around to see me. Her kidneys are rotten; she sells half her medicine to buy me things, gifts she brings. She tells me, 'Thank God I have kidney disease; it's the only way I could make money.' I'm killing her slowly. What kind of hero does that make me? A hero waiting to be exchanged with another prisoner. An exchange that will never happen. The only way it could happen is if my blood turns black, expires, ages. I'll be exchanged when I'm completely humiliated. Not humiliated by my jailer, no, the jailer doesn't have that power over me. My humiliation feeds on watching *haja* Salma, selling her blood for my sake. Fuck the prisoner exchange. Fuck it.

SLAP (*entering*). Your mosquito is on my shoulder. Take her.

MOSQUITO *puts the mosquito back in the matchbox.* SLAP *takes out his notebook and begins writing.*

The time for lying is over. I'll write what I didn't write before, what no poet or author has penned before. You'll be surprised to learn that I went outside, I went at thirteen hundred hours outside the prison… There was a real bus. Suddenly the bus starting spluttering, the engine putting out smoke and sparks flew through the bars of the front grill… I felt a danger coming… I went to the bus driver and asked him, 'What's wrong?' Said to me, 'The motor is dead,' so I slapped him black and blue. One of the prisoners stood up and started crying, 'Our happiness is not meant to be.' I slapped him so hard, his teeth popped. The other prisoners started gathering them from the floor. The guard looked at me with fear in his eyes. He said, 'Due to a technical error, the prisoner exchange has been delayed till tomorrow…' I laughed a mocking laugh… 'Ha, ha, ha…' then I slapped him and told him… 'Tomorrow is Friday and I'd like to rest… leave it till the day after… then on my way – '

MOSQUITO. Come on, man! The mosquito is dying of hunger.

SLAP. Leave me be or I'll slap you so hard, you'll see stars at noon.

MOSQUITO. Boxman is lost, Snake is not talking to me because I hit him… there's no else left but you.

SLAP. I hate your mosquito… I hate all insects… I've no blood left in me.

MOSQUITO. Yes, you have.

SLAP. No, I don't.

MOSQUITO. She's got nothing but your blood and mine to suck on.

SLAP. My blood is contaminated by all the medication I've been taking. It won't do.

MOSQUITO. She got used to it.

SLAP. Get away from me or I'll slap you so hard, blood will pour out of your eyes.

MOSQUITO *takes out a letter from his shirt.*

What's that?

MOSQUITO. Your story… your diary… not the stories about 'I slapped him' and 'He slapped me' where you are the hero, but the other kind, the stories you write while we sleep… and there I was thinking you're writing about Marx and Lenin.

SLAP. Where'd you find it?

MOSQUITO. None of your business… Give me your hand.

SLAP. I won't.

MOSQUITO (*starts reading*). They've imposed a curfew… gathered the men on one side and the women on the other.

SLAP. Don't, Mosquito.

MOSQUITO. The soldier shouted at the men. 'Sit down on your arse now!'

SLAP. Stop, Mosquito. Please.

MOSQUITO. They all sat on their arses except Slap… The soldier looked at him and said, 'Hey, you, on your arse, now!' I told him I wasn't going to do it. The soldier got angry and told his commanding officer that 'this animal' refuses to sit down. The officer told me, 'I'll massacre this entire village if you don't sit down on your arse right now.' The villagers panicked, their elders began screaming at Slap to sit down.

SLAP. Enough, Mosquito. Don't finish it.

MOSQUITO. And the women beat their heads and screamed, 'God curse you, Slap, you want to widow us for the sake of your arse?' The officer slapped me so hard I saw the stars of noon. He fired rounds between my feet. I screamed, 'In the name of Allah, don't shoot! I've got piles, that's why I can't sit down!' Everyone began to laugh… I was humiliated.

SLAP. Enough, Mosquito.

MOSQUITO. I became the butt of all jokes in the village. 'Here comes the piles man.' 'There goes the piles man.' Even when I found a girl and wanted her hand in marriage…

SLAP *snatches the matchbox from* MOSQUITO *and puts it between his feet.* MOSQUITO *approaches him.*

SLAP. You take one more step and I'll squash her... turn her to powder... to dust... blood will pour out of her eyes... as it did from mine, when you were reading just now.

MOSQUITO. Don't do it, Slap.

SLAP. Go on... Continue... I went seeking the hand of the girl. Her father told me, 'We're not marrying her to a joke like you; her groom must have a sound arse.'

SLAP*'s foot gets closer to the matchbox.*

MOSQUITO. For God's sake.

SLAP. I asked to be transferred to another school in another village; they transferred me to a garbage heap... a broken man.

MOSQUITO. You've never been broken... You were the man who slapped the soldier and put him in the hospital for a month.

SLAP*'s foot gets closer still to the matchbox.*

SLAP. I slapped him by accident... I didn't do it out of patriotic duty... I've never given our nation a moment's thought in my life.

MOSQUITO. I'm begging you, don't do it.

SLAP. Fuck the nation. Fuck this country. Look how much blood it has demanded from us... and for what? For dirt and rocks and stones and orchards... Fuck all these things... I want to live... I want to hear the other and have him hear me... not slap and be slapped back... forgive and be for-given... not hit and be beaten... Fuck this country for all the blood it took... I want to hold this country by the scruff and slap it across the face... slap its greens and yellows... slap Marx and Lenin, slap and slap and slap.

SLAP *goes into a fit and smashes the matchbox.*

MOSQUITO. What've you done?

*He runs to the box, trying to rescue the mosquito.*

You've trampled on my soul.

*SNAKE carries SLAP and puts him on bed. SLAP remains in the grip of the fit till the end due to absence of medicine. SNAKE grabs the matchbox and begins tapping on it until the mosquito returns.*

*The light begins to dim till darkness.*

*Suddenly we hear the horn of a bus loudly. The sound is deafening. The metal door opens.*

*We see SIREN in the corner, wrapped in a white dress, spinning in circles.*

*A voice comes over the loudspeakers saying in Hebrew:*

VOICE. Prisoner 2002, known as Mosquito. You are released.

Prisoner 607, known as Slap. You are released.

Prisoner 301, known as Boxman. You are released.

*This is repeated several times.*

*No one exits.*

*SNAKE heads towards the door. He looks at the exit then suddenly runs out.*

SIREN. Wait.

*Lights down quickly and completely.*

*The End.*

**DAMAGE**

عطب

KAMAL KHALLADI

*translated by*

HOUDA ECHOUAFNI

## Kamal Khalladi

Kamal Khalladi is a playwright, director, university course director and founding member of the Théâtre de l'Atelier in Meknes, Morocco. Previous work as a writer/director includes *Cancer*, *Rue Eugene UNESCO No. 27*, *Tjakhmira* and *Comedia*. His adaptations include *Iham w ifham* by Saadlah Wanouss and *Tkarkib nabb* by Y.A. Alamy.

## Houda Echouafni

Houda Echouafni is an actress of Moroccan/Egyptian descent. Her screen acting credits include *The Grid* (Fox Television Network); *The Mark of Cain*, *The Death of Klinghoffer* and *Green Wing* (Channel 4); *Waking the Dead*, *Hotel Babylon*, *Doctors*, *Dirty War* and *Sea of Souls* (BBC); and the films *Les oiseaux du ciel* (Canal+) and *31 North 62 East*. Theatre work includes *Plan D* (Tristan Bates Theatre, London), *The Duchess of Malfi* (Jermyn Street Theatre, London), *Change* (Assembly Rooms, Edinburgh) and *Leaving Home* (The King's Head, London).

*Damage* was first performed as a rehearsed reading as part of the *I Come From There: New Plays from the Arab World* season in the Jerwood Theatre Upstairs, Royal Court Theatre, London, on 13 November 2008, with the following cast:

| | |
|---|---|
| YOUSSEF | Al Nedjari |
| SANA'A | Houda Echouafni |
| MUM | Amira Ghazalla |
| COLONEL | Raad Rawi |
| MOURAD ALZAHZOUHI | Khalid Laith |
| HAMID BOUZIDI | Munir Khairdin |
| SHANDOURAI | Simone James |
| YANKA | Michelle Asante |
| TAMARA | Yetunde Oduwole |
| JOSEPH DIWI | Jude Akuwudike |
| *Director* | Ramin Gray |

The play was also read at Masrah Al Madina in Beirut, Lebanon, in January 2009.

**Characters**

YOUSSEF, *Lieutenant, thirties*
SANA'A, *Youssef's wife, late twenties*
MUM, *Sana'a's mum, late forties*
COLONEL, *mid-fifties*
MOURAD ALZAHZOUHI, *Lieutenant*
HAMID BOUZIDI, *Lieutenant*
SHANDOURAI, *African girl, twenties*
YANKA, *African girl, twenties*
TAMARA, *African girl, twenties*
JOSEPH DIWI, *an old African man, staying at the MONUC-run medical tent*

**Settings**

A flat on the third floor, El Madina El Jadida, Meknes, Morocco. A living room, a sofa, TV, and a low coffee table. We are able to see a balcony through the living room, through two wooden doors.

A corridor leading to a door through which we see a large mirror.

The Colonel's office: table and chairs, TV.

A small basement room in the soldiers' quarters of MONUC in the Bunia area in the Congo.

A field near MONUC. We can see a large African tree.

## Notes and references

*Agadir* – a tourist town, home to the largest military base in Southern Morocco. It is the starting point for soldiers to the Sahara, as well as sub-Saharan Africa.

*Khénifra* – a town known for prostitution

*Meknes* – a city in northern Morocco, it was the imperial capital of Morocco under the reign of Moulay Ismail. It has the biggest army academy in Morocco. The city is split into an old town and a new town

*MONUC* – the UN peacekeeping mission in the Congo

*Polisario* – a Sahrawi rebel-liberation movement working for the independence of Western Sahara from Morocco. There was an ongoing armed conflict between the Polisario and Morocco throughout the 1970s and 1980s, ending in a ceasefire agreement in 1991, though the Western Sahara remains a disputed territory.

**Scene One**

*In the* COLONEL*'s office.* YOUSSEF, HAMID *and* MOURAD.

HAMID (*to* YOUSSEF). You need to make a decision, man.

MOURAD. Just mind your own business, yeah?

HAMID. So, you think you can tell him what to do?

MOURAD. Don't listen to that prick, if he knew any better he'd still be married.

YOUSSEF. Where are they sending us?

MOURAD. Bosnia, thirteen days since the last soldiers came back, so...

HAMID. Fancy yourself some blond cock do you?

   MOURAD *attacks* HAMID, YOUSSEF *breaks it up. We get the sense that this is a running joke.*

YOUSSEF. Enough!

HAMID (*not giving up*). Don't worry, wherever we end up, I'll find someone to fuck you.

   *They attack each other. The door opens. The* COLONEL *enters, the three* SOLDIERS *straighten up, get in position and salute.*

COLONEL. A fiery lot, I like it, the Congo is perfect for you.

YOUSSEF. The Congo?

COLONEL. Problem?

YOUSSEF. No, Colonel.

   COLONEL *approaches* MOURAD, *strokes his cheek.*

COLONEL. The Congo is where you want to be, it'll toughen you up, you're too green. A real soldier needs to look weathered, he needs a thick hide.

*He moves on to* HAMID, *notices something on his uniform.*

Married?

MOURAD. Divorced.

COLONEL. It shows. (*To* YOUSSEF.) Married?

YOUSSEF. Yes, Colonel.

COLONEL. How long?

YOUSSEF. Three weeks.

COLONEL. I see… You know you can ask to be excused, there are plenty of soldiers ready to take your place.

YOUSSEF *doesn't answer.*

A real soldier never hesitates.

YOUSSEF. Sir, am I allowed to ask a question?

COLONEL. I'm listening.

YOUSSEF. How much do we get paid?

COLONEL. 4,500 DH a month.

YOUSSEF. I'm prepared to serve, sir.

COLONEL. That's what I like to see, men willing to take the bull by the horns. Well done, my son, you all remind me of my youth when I used to flit around. This is what a soldier is. He does not own himself. If a place offers me a new experience, I'd jump and land right in the middle of it. I never felt anything called 'fear'. (*Lights a cigar.*) I tried to leave a hand or a foot somewhere. But I couldn't. That's a medal I didn't achieve in the army.

In Africa, life deserves to be lived, live it.

You are going to the heart of Africa. Enjoy life, open your eyes, unlock your hearts. Lieutenant Hamid, I heard about the trouble you caused in the local club last night.

HAMID. Colonel…

COLONEL. Stay away from young girls, do you hear me? In Africa, you'll find passionate women, not little girls, women who know how to move, know how to satisfy your wildest fantasies. Ever tasted black meat, boys…? Fucking delicious.

When you secure the Congo and enter the capital, the Congolese women will throw themselves at you just like the French women threw themselves at the Moroccan liberators after the World War. Then you'll feel like real soldiers, real men. Lieutenant Youssef, when you're away, your wife will miss you, she'll hunger for you, you wait till you get back… her passion will blow your mind.

Don't forget now, you will be representing this great country, we are the peacekeepers, understand?

Any questions?

MOURAD. How long are we gonna be posted there, sir?

COLONEL. Nine months.

HAMID. When do we leave, sir?

COLONEL. In forty-eight hours.

*He picks up some papers from his desk.*

These are your train tickets to Agadir, there will be seven hundred of you, from there you board a plane to the Congo. Don't overpack, everything you need is there. Remember, you represent Morocco, our reputation is in your hands.

*They salute and exit.*

**Scene Two**

*The flat.* YOUSSEF *is smoking,* SANA'A *enters from outside.*

SANA'A. Hello, stinky… enough of these cigarettes… How many times have I told you to at least let some air in…?

*She opens the doors to the balcony.*

Give me your foot, you lazy bum.

SANA'A *pulls* YOUSSEF'*s leg until he falls to the floor. She laughs and starts undoing his laces.*

How was your day?

YOUSSEF. Same as usual.

SANA'A. Tell me something.

YOUSSEF. I have nothing to tell.

SANA'A. I don't care, you are the one who got me used to it.

YOUSSEF. Grow up.

SANA'A. I don't wanna grow up… Come on… tell me!

YOUSSEF. Honestly… I can't find anything to tell.

SANA'A. Fine, next time… when you've got nothing to tell, lie a really good lie, spice it up and I'll believe you, okay? Guess what…? Today at the gym I was getting changed for class and I noticed that both my socks had holes in them, everyone was staring at me and I felt so embarrassed, then I thought, 'Fuck it' – you should have seen me in class, they couldn't keep up with me… Okay, now your turn.

YOUSSEF. All right, but you won't like what I have to say.

SANA'A. Then keep it to yourself.

YOUSSEF. You need to know.

SANA'A. What? Is it going to make me cry?

YOUSSEF. Not sure, I just know you won't like it.

SANA'A. How about this? If I start crying just tickle my tummy.

YOUSSEF. I am going to serve in the Congo.

SANA'A. Ha ha, very funny, pull the other one.

YOUSSEF. I am not joking, the Colonel told me today.

SANA'A. You're serious…? What do we have to do with the Congo?!

YOUSSEF. War has broken out there so Morocco is sending its army.

SANA'A. You are not going!!

YOUSSEF. Sana'a!

SANA'A. This is bullshit, three weeks we've been married, it's bullshit! Look, tomorrow when you see the Colonel, ask him to excuse you.

YOUSSEF. And the reason?

SANA'A. Personal reasons. 'I just got married. I can't leave my wife on her own and go to the Congo. My wife is sick…'

YOUSSEF. This isn't school. I am a soldier. I knew what was in store when I chose to join.

SANA'A. The Colonel will understand.

YOUSSEF. The Colonel has no say in this.

SANA'A. We can speak to Baba's friends in Rabat, they won't say no to me.

YOUSSEF. This is my job. A soldier obeys orders, it's shameful for a soldier to say no.

SANA'A. Yeah? And it's not shameful to remove a soldier from his wife's bed when they've only been married for three weeks?

YOUSSEF. This is my job. You know that.

SANA'A. I know you're a soldier in Morocco, not the Congo.

YOUSSEF. Morocco or the Congo… a soldier is a soldier.

*Beat.*

SANA'A. And how long will you stay there?

YOUSSEF. Nine months. Look, Sana'a, we are drowning in debt, a mission like this means I'll get paid 4,500 DH plus my salary.

SANA'A. When did we care about money? Have I ever complained? Do you need anything? You are talking as if you want to go of your own free will.

YOUSSEF. I put in the request to go. I did not know that my luck was going to land me in the Congo.

SANA'A. You did what? Without telling me, without asking me, as if I don't exist, I am not part of the equation, right? You should have just said that they are sending you and stopped there. I would have forgotten, I would have let it go, understood… Lie to me, lie to me and say, 'They are sending me,' lie to me and say, 'I don't want to go.'

YOUSSEF. There comes a time when a man has to choose!

SANA'A. *We* need to choose.

YOUSSEF. It's all the same.

SANA'A. Maybe for you, but sure as hell not for me! Do you know what war in the Congo means? You know how death sweeps there? You know how weapons are handed out like sweets? You know tsetse, the plague, cholera, Ebola? Do you not know what Ebola is?

YOUSSEF. We are going to be immunised before we leave.

SANA'A. Don't lie to yourself. When Ebola hits, a person becomes like a sack of blood, blood seeps out from the nose, the mouth, the eyes, from the back, front, from the inside and out, blood can pierce the skin and pour out like a sieve.

YOUSSEF. That's it! Enough. Do you understand what it means to be a soldier?

SANA'A. Soldier, soldier, soldier. What is a soldier? An idiot who jumps in the fire with his eyes open, that's a soldier, yeah?

*Beat.*

YOUSSEF. We need to live like everyone else, be like other people, walk like them and talk like them.

SANA'A. What the hell are you on about?

YOUSSEF. I am on about the fact that Jamal, Mr Director of the Electricity Board, has pockets stuffed full of cash. He's cosy. I'm just a soldier, fresh out of the academy. 'A soldier is like a cuckoo, he never builds a nest.' Isn't that what your mum said?

SANA'A. This subject is over.

YOUSSEF. No, it isn't. We can't just sweep things under the rug. Your mum wants you to have the car, the villa and a healthy bank account. For people to respect us and let us live amongst them we have to have that villa, that car and that healthy bank account. Listen, every country has its own Ebola, there are different types. There's a type of Ebola that heads straight for the soul, it grinds it, and wrings it and knocks a man down to the ground. Your mum's words are a form of Ebola.

SANA'A. This isn't you talking… Enough about Mama, the Director of the Electricity Board, and the Congo. Let's just live together, just the two of us. You are the one who told me that real and pure things always happen between two people, from the third only comes chaos. We don't need the house, the car, the bank account. Let's just hold on to each other so we don't get lost in the crowd.

YOUSSEF. Your words are beautiful… but I need to go… (*Beat.*) You need to get back in touch with your mum.

SANA'A. What?

YOUSSEF. I don't want you to be on your own.

SANA'A. You're the last person to want her in our lives!

YOUSSEF. What she did to me isn't important. I don't want you to be on your own.

SANA'A. If I let her back into our lives… I don't even want to think about it.

YOUSSEF. I know, but your mum is still better than a stranger.

SANA'A. You have nothing to worry about.

YOUSSEF. And another thing…

SANA'A. Stop it, all this talk is scaring me.

YOUSSEF. What are you scared of?

SANA'A. What's coming.

YOUSSEF. An amazing life together is coming, silly. I can't wait till I go and come back so we can make a beautiful baby girl that will look like her mama. What shall we call her?

SANA'A. Wait till she's born, then we can talk about naming her.

YOUSSEF. No, I want to name her now.

SANA'A. Youssef.

YOUSSEF. Sana'a.

SANA'A. We can name her… Maisa?

YOUSSEF. Nice… And if it's a boy… ?

SANA'A. You tell me.

YOUSSEF. How about Almahdy?

SANA'A. Deal!

YOUSSEF. Soldier, weapon, salute.

SANA'A. Youssef.

YOUSSEF. Soldier, weapon, salute.

SANA'A. Yes, my Lieutenant.

*They kiss.*

## Scene Three

*The flat.* SANA'A *enters, she has come back from the market. She throws down her shopping basket, she unwraps a framed picture of* YOUSSEF *and starts talking to it.*

SANA'A. It's like the whole town knows you're away. It's like they can smell that I'm on my own.

The guy at number 18 who's just bought a new car keeps asking me if I want a ride. The last time he tried it on I let him get away with too much, I could tell he was up to something, he got too close and said, 'If I had a woman like you I wouldn't leave the flat, let alone the country.' What do you think I should've done? Spat at him? Oh, I did, then what?

I'm scared I'll wake up one day and find him spooning me.

I'm weak and empty, you're gonna come back and find nothing left.

Oh, by the way, those plants you left keep wilting no matter how much I water them.

*The doorbell rings,* SANA'A *opens the door to find her mother.*

MUM. How are you?

SANA'A. Good.

SANA'A *moves and lets her* MUM *in.*

MUM. Your stairs almost gave me a heart attack…

SANA'A. The lift is broken, no one in the building wants to pay to get it fixed.

MUM. What's the matter? You don't look well.

SANA'A. I've had a bad day, that's all.

MUM. When is he coming back?

SANA'A. His name is Youssef.

MUM. Sure… When is he coming back?

SANA'A. In nine months… You know, it was Youssef who asked me to call you.

MUM. Strange.

SANA'A. Youssef has a good heart…

MUM. I am thirsty.

SANA'A. What would you like?

MUM. Have you got anything ready?

SANA'A. Black coffee?

MUM. So you haven't given that up yet?

SANA'A. I can make you something else.

MUM. No, never mind… I'll take a small cup.

SANA'A *goes to prepare the coffee,* MUM *walks around the flat.*

Can I see your bedroom?

SANA'A. It's locked.

MUM. Tell me where the key is. I'll open it.

SANA'A. I don't have the key.

MUM. Who has it?

SANA'A. Youssef.

MUM. So, where do you sleep?

SANA'A. It depends, anywhere else, really.

MUM. Why did he take the key?

SANA'A. I asked him to.

MUM. Why?

SANA'A. I can't go in the bedroom without Youssef.

MUM. Well, at least allow the room to breathe a little.

SANA'A. When Youssef gets back, there will be plenty of time to air it and let it breathe.

MUM. You will find it full of damp.

SANA'A. Doesn't matter.

*Beat.*

MUM. There are still a lot of things missing in your flat.

SANA'A. We'll get them in our own time, there's no rush.

MUM. What's Youssef's salary?

SANA'A. I didn't ask.

MUM. You don't know? Or you don't want to say?

SANA'A. That's none of your business.

MUM. Don't be silly. Of course it is, it's my right to know if you are taken care of.

SANA'A. Please mind your own business.

MUM. Sweetheart, I only want what's best for you.

SANA'A *switches the TV on. They sit in silence.*

## Scene Four

*The basement room, a low table, lots of empty alcohol bottles, a packets of cigarettes and ashtrays.* MOURAD *and* YOUSSEF.

MOURAD. You're smoking like a chimney.

YOUSSEF. Only thing keeping me going.

MOURAD. Do you know what you need?

YOUSSEF. No, but you're gonna tell me anyway.

MOURAD. It's just that Hamid mentioned some Ukrainian girls…

YOUSSEF *laughs*.

Between you and me, I prefer black meat, remember what the Colonel said…

YOUSSEF. Yeah…

MOURAD. So? What should we order?

YOUSSEF. Not hungry, mate.

HAMID *enters*.

HAMID. The girls are on their way, you better be up for it.

YOUSSEF. What girls?

HAMID. The black girls, have you ever had a black girl, bruv?

MOURAD. Who the fuck told you to get any girls?

HAMID. Oh shit, sorry, man, I should've asked for a little boy for you.

MOURAD. You should've asked for your sister.

HAMID (*laughs*). You can't handle her.

MOURAD. Yeah? Try me.

HAMID *throws* MOURAD *three condoms*.

HAMID. If you prove yourself today, I promise, I'll bring her to you myself.

*Throws a condom to* YOUSSEF.

Youssef, don't be so boring, man, have a little taste. You'll feel better.

MOURAD. Yeah, come on, man, let's forget about this hellhole we're in for a couple of hours at least.

YOUSSEF. I am saying this once. No girl is coming in.

HAMID. Sooner or later, you'll realise marriage isn't for soldiers. How do you know what your wife is up to?

*YOUSSEF attacks HAMID, MOURAD breaks it up.*

Listen, bruv, I don't wanna hurt you. I'll let your wife do that.

*Takes a beer bottle and downs it.*

I was only away for a month, I walked in and found my wife sucking cock on my bed, bruv, in my bed...

So, fuck away, who knows... that leg the Belgian lost today could've been yours... or mine. (*Pointing to HAMID.*) Or even yours, pussy.

*Starts laughing, his laugh mingles with new laughter from the girls outside.*

Let's show them what the Moroccans are made of...

*Three local girls enter – SHANDOURAI, YANKA and TAMARA. African music starts playing.*

MOURAD (*smacks YANKA's backside*). Yeah, man...

YANKA (*exposing her bum cheek*). Kiss that.

*MOURAD does so with pleasure.*

HAMID (*to MOURAD*). Live, man.

*Puts his arms around TAMARA as he kisses SHAN-DOURAI.*

You... Dance for us.

*Pushing SHANDOURAI to dance.*

Dance for us.

*SHANDOURAI, the youngest and most attractive, seems hesitant. TAMARA hands her a glass, she downs it and starts dancing.*

MOURAD. Nah... I don't like that dance, do a different one.

SHANDOURAI. Sorry, I can't... I'm a bit tired.

MOURAD. I said, I want another dance.

HAMID. You are here to do what we ask, not what you want...
get it?

YANKA. I can dance for you. You'll like what I've got.

HAMID. I want her to dance.

*He grabs* SHANDOURAI*'s arm.*

YOUSSEF. The girl said she's tired.

HAMID. I'm not paying her to be tired.

YOUSSEF. Be a man.

HAMID. You be a man.

MOURAD. Don't upset our brother Youssef, he's a one-woman
man.

HAMID. You like her, don't you...?

*He pushes* SHANDOURAI *towards* YOUSSEF.

Here, just make sure you fuck her. (*To* YANKA.) You...
Show me that dance.

YANKA *takes her shirt off and starts dancing in her bra.*

And this dance is called Viagra.

MOURAD. Remember what the Colonel said...

HAMID. Black meat...

MOURAD. Is something else...

HAMID. That bastard knew what he was talking about.

YOUSSEF (*to* SHANDOURAI). Your dance was... depressing.

SHANDOURAI. My soul is depressed, nothing will change that
in the Congo... Give me a cigarette.

YOUSSEF *lights* SHANDOURAI*'s cigarette.*

You're kind... Your friends are having a good time.

YOUSSEF. They're drunk.

SHANDOURAI. You don't want to touch me.

YOUSSEF. No.

SHANDOURAI. You don't find me attractive.

YOUSSEF. I do.

SHANDOURAI. So, what's the problem…? Oh! Sorry, I get it, you don't like women.

YOUSSEF. I don't like whores.

SHANDOURAI. I wasn't insulting you… A lot of soldiers like their pretty boys.

YOUSSEF. Sorry for snapping at you.

SHANDOURAI. Oh, please… I've heard it plenty.

YOUSSEF. You didn't tell me your name.

SHANDOURAI. Shandourai.

YOUSSEF. That's pretty.

SHANDOURAI. You?

YOUSSEF. Youssef.

SHANDOURAI. That's like Joseph.

YOUSSEF. Yeah.

SHANDOURAI. God, it's hot, mind if I take my shirt off?

YOUSSEF. Sure.

> SHANDOURAI *takes her shirt off and sits closer to*
> YOUSSEF. *She takes a picture out of her bra.*

SHANDOURAI. This is my husband, he's dead, killed actually, his name was Karoumi, he was my professor before… Karoumi was famous, you know, even in the capital, his picture was always in the papers. He had a lot of white friends, one day, he came home and told me he's about to shame the criminals… Give me another cigarette!

YOUSSEF *lights a cigarette for* SHANDOURAI *and one for him.*

Thanks.

*Beat.*

Here's a little anecdote for you. His assassin was his room-mate at university. They accused him of high treason then decapitated him.

*Silence.*

YOUSSEF. What's going to happen to you?

SHANDOURAI. Cross the border... kiss me... I said kiss me!

*He kisses her.*

Fuck me!

### Scene Five

*The flat.* SANA'A *is sitting by the balcony.* MUM *enters, adjusting her clothes and her hair, and drinking a glass of milk.*

SANA'A. I can't fall asleep!

MUM. I used to wait by the balcony myself. It's part of the army wife's curse... waiting.

SANA'A. You used to stand on the balcony waiting for Baba?

MUM. For a long time... Eventually I got used to sleeping alone.

SANA'A. I don't think I'll ever get used to that.

MUM. I know... It's much harder for women.

SANA'A. What do you mean?

MUM. Men don't really care, especially soldiers, a soldier will bury his face in the first chest he finds.

SANA'A. Where do you get this hate for soldiers from?

MUM. Like you don't know.

SANA'A. I don't.

MUM. Your baba, where else?

SANA'A. Don't... He was a good man.

MUM. To you.

SANA'A. To everyone.

MUM. You think you know him? How could you when you only saw him for ten days every three months?

SANA'A. Baba was killing himself in the desert so we can have a good life.

MUM (*laughs*). Us and the prostitutes of Khénifra.

SANA'A. What the hell are you talking about now?

MUM. Your baba used to come to me after he had been sucked dry. After three months of being away his first stop was always the whores of Khénifra, and he only came to us after he ran out of money.

SANA'A. Oh my God... you know I'm never going to believe that.

MUM. I know... That's why I'm not going to tell you about all the other things, but this you should know: he didn't even want me to have children, if I hadn't stopped the pill in secret you wouldn't be here right now.

SANA'A. What?

MUM. You heard me.

SANA'A. You can make up any shit, he's not here to defend himself.

MUM. I never wanted you to know any of this...

I just don't want you to suffer like I did. I want to open your eyes to the fact that black girls in the Congo are a penny a dozen. Who knows, he might catch something there and pass it on to you. Do you remember the Captain who used to live above? He went to the Congo... Did you see his skin...?

SANA'A. Youssef would never cheat on me...

MUM. Did he say that? They're all the same. Your dad worshipped the ground I walked on, until he started getting promoted... The minute he started earning some proper money, off he went to the strippers and the whores.

SANA'A. Oh, sure... You probably made his life hell.

MUM. When will you realise that they take out all the crap they see on women?

SANA'A. And when will you realise that soldiers are like everyone else, you have the good and the bad.

MUM. They are all the same, they don't give them that uniform until they kill their souls.

*Beat.*

Have you ever wondered why you're an only child?

*Silence.*

You know you used to moan about it when you were little... I can tell you now if you want?

*Silence.*

I couldn't, I had a hysterectomy.

SANA'A. Some bedtime story I'm getting tonight.

MUM. I am here to tell you everything... I need you to know.

Your baba was late coming back once, later than usual, it had been four months since he left and there was talk amongst the wives that the Polisario had captured some soldiers, so I went to see the Colonel to check.

I don't know how it happened, we were talking... then he started undoing my buttons... he looked me in the eyes and said, 'That's better, you can breathe now...' One thing led to another... Anyway, he told me to come back the next day and he'll find out about your baba.

When I got home, I was shocked at myself, I couldn't believe what I did... with your baba's friend of all people. I decided not to go back the next day.

Three days I locked myself in the flat, I didn't even go out for groceries... I gave in on the fourth day, I went to see him, knowing full well that I wasn't going for news.

As soon as I walked in he handed me keys to his flat and told me the address... We started meeting there every day...

SANA'A. Did you like it?

*Beat.*

Answer me.

MUM. Yes.

SANA'A. Aren't you ashamed of yourself?

MUM. I couldn't help myself, he lit a fire in me I had forgotten was even there. I started falling for him.

Anyway, soon after that, I woke up with a fever and the worst rash you can imagine. A doctor came and took one look down there and told me it was an STD. When I told the Colonel he became hysterical, took him some time to calm down. Finally he admitted he'd picked up something from God knows where.

That day he took his keys back, threw some money at me, and kicked me out.

I kept taking the medicine but it was no use, the doctor said I had to...

Your baba had no idea, how could he, he was never here long enough.

So, you see…?

*Beat.*

It can happen to anyone… you included, if you don't change things.

SANA'A. What do you mean? 'Change things'?

MUM. Ask for a divorce now, before you're stuck with kids.

SANA'A. He won't divorce me.

MUM. You can go to court.

SANA'A. The court can't do anything about it, he's in the army.

MUM. You don't need to worry about it, Jamal will take care of everything.

SANA'A. Did he put you up to this?

MUM. Yes… he's still in love with you.

You are so much better off with him, trust me. He is the Director of the Electricity Board, that means something… You'll live in a villa, have the latest car, shop till you drop and bathe in French perfume…

So… what do you think?

SANA'A. I think I regret calling you. Are you crazy? What am I…? A prostitute who swaps husbands like she swaps knickers?

You are nothing to me… not any more.

SANA'A *switches the lights off.*

## Scene Six

*The flat. The doorbell rings,* SANA'A *hurries to open it. She returns with a letter, and starts to read it in front of the large mirror in the hallway. We begin hearing it in* YOUSSEF's *voice.*

YOUSSEF (*voice-over*). My darling Sana'a –

I miss you, from the moment my feet touched the Congo, all I've done is miss you. The weather here is dusty and boiling. The heat makes everything seem blurry, the sky is red, the land is red, the red dust covers everything, swallows you in dirt and fire. Water heated up by the sun doesn't help get rid of the dirt, the heat makes the blood boil and come out of your nose. I am in Itori, in a town called Bunia, there is a lot of work to be done, we are slowly clearing the landmines.

MUM. What's wrong? You're as white as a sheet.

SANA'A. Nothing, nothing's wrong.

SANA'A *continues reading.*

YOUSSEF (*voice-over*). I miss your beautiful laugh, I miss those gorgeous afternoons that were our gift from early summer. I miss morning breakfast, morning kisses and morning coffee. The past tense here is a necessary form of protection. I beg you, write me a lot. I was eating those sweets you sent, one of my friends had a bite and said, 'These sweets were made with pure love, send some more.' We get post here every fortnight, you can send stuff via the Colonel's office.

SANA'A *laughs and runs into one of the rooms.*

MUM. Listen to him and his well-thought-out words... (*Raising her voice so* SANA'A *can hear.*) Words are neither here nor there, if words cost money you would be staring at a blank page.

SANA'A *comes back with a video camera, a flowery dress that she puts on. She switches the camera on, sets it on a tripod and starts speaking directly to it.*

SANA'A. Hi, Youssef… I miss you, how are you? I got your
letter today, it made me so happy, I wanted to remind you of
me – Ta-dah! Hope you like it, what shall I tell you…? I
don't know how to start. A kiss first. Okay, how shall I
start… How shall I start…? I am going to remind you of the
first time we went out.

MUM *goes into the bedroom, putting her hands over her ears.*

It was the first time we sat close together… Do you
remember? It was in a taxi. It was the beginning of summer,
as we got in it had just started drizzling. I was wearing this
very dress. I know you like it on me.

I was wet, happy and waiting for something, I kept saying to
myself, 'Open your heart, Sana'a, genuinely open it.' So I
opened my heart and my soul.

Inside, the restaurant was quiet. The diners were barely
moving their lips. You took me to that table in the corner, it
was particularly dark, I knew you wanted to get closer.

You had the sleeves of your shirt rolled up, your arms white
and full of thick black hair. For a long while we didn't speak,
then you asked me if I liked the restaurant. Again we drowned
in silence, my blood was boiling, I found you to be infuriating,
God how infuriating, don't get angry. Here… another kiss.

But really you were infuriating.

You filled my head with questions. You made me doubt
everything. I asked you if we should leave, I was hoping you
would say, 'It's too early, I don't want to leave you, we
didn't talk much,' something along those lines.

Before I finished my sentence, you stood up. I heard the
sound of your boots hitting one another. You paid and stood
by the door. I was dragging my feet in my kitten heels, not
sure if I should hurry or slow down. Then we stood waiting
for a taxi that took for ever. You sat with me in the back,
when you reached over to shut the door that I didn't shut
properly, I noticed your hand trembling, and you had goose-
bumps. I felt sorry for you. We got out of the taxi, I still had

a little patience left, my heart and soul were still open. You said, 'Forgive me, Sana'a, I didn't say much, actually I said nothing. But I enjoyed your company.'

I was so, so happy.

Oh, those words! Where did you find them?

I sat by the phone all week waiting for you to call.

Yesterday, while I was taking a shower the gas cylinder finished, the water turned cold. I spent the whole day freezing. Morocco beat the Senegal three – nil.

(*Gets a newspaper.*) Here, listen to what I read in the newspaper yesterday, I was looking for a job to fill the time and found this.

(*Reading from newspaper.*) 'A team of researchers in North Carolina has concluded that a woman's embrace causes an increase in the levels of the oxytocin hormone, which is also known as the attraction hormone. It also decreases the levels of the cortisol hormone, which has the positive affect of stabilising blood pressure, which in turn decreases the likelihood of heart-related illnesses. Karen Germaine, the researcher behind the study, advises all the couples in the world to go ahead and embrace some more.'

According to this, my heart should have shrivelled and my arteries turned to stone.

I am just joking, your soldier is as constant as ever.

MUM *appears with her suitcase.*

I miss you, Youssef, I miss you so much, I miss you.

If I had you right now I would rip you apart.

*Kisses him.*

Mama's staying with me, I called her like you asked, she's changed a lot, she really likes you now.

MUM *goes to the camera and gives it the finger, she heads towards the door. We hear it slam.*

## Scene Seven

*The* COLONEL*'s office. The* COLONEL *is smoking a cigar. He presses a button, the door opens.*

COLONEL. Come on in.

SANA'A. Thank you.

*She sits.*

COLONEL. Would you like something to drink?

SANA'A. No thanks.

COLONEL. You must have something to drink. How about some lemonade?

SANA'A. I'll take a black coffee if it's not too much trouble.

COLONEL. For you, anything.

*Puts a capsule in the coffee machine and a cup.*

Do you always drink black coffee?

SANA'A. A bad habit from my college days.

COLONEL. Coffee is good and bad. It must be consumed in moderation. Would you like me to put out the cigar?

SANA'A. No, not at all. I only came about a package. I am not going to take much of your time.

COLONEL. Not a problem. It's not often beautiful women like yourself visit us.

SANA'A. That's too kind.

COLONEL. I'm simply stating a fact.

SANA'A. I am Lieutenant Youssef Wakrem's wife.

COLONEL. From the three that left our brigade to the Congo. They're three of our best. You're Commander Nabil's daughter, correct?

SANA'A. Yes. How did you know, Colonel?

COLONEL. I signed your marriage authorisation. Your father was a great man. You know, I spent a month with him in the Sahara. He has taught me much. Your baba could never stop talking about you. So you see, I knew you since you were a little girl running around in pigtails, and look at you now, a complete woman. You have a magnificent presence. You remind me of the original stars of the silver screen, stars like Ingrid Bergman, Romy Schneider, Lana Turner. Do you like the cinema?

SANA'A. Yes, actually I was the founder of the Cinema Club at college.

COLONEL. So, no doubt you have seen *Casablanca*?

SANA'A. Of course!

COLONEL. I have watched it at least thirty times. Do you remember the scene where Ilsa goes to Rick at night to ask him to help her and her husband escape to Lisbon? Ingrid was breathtaking.

SANA'A. Yeah, I like that scene, but my favourite is right at the end, when he goes with them to the airport... completely heartbreaking.

COLONEL. One day I'll invite you to come and see a film with me. You are an amazing woman. Youssef Wakrem is lucky to have you.

SANA'A. Don't forget, Colonel, that Lieutenant Youssef Wakrem is a deserving man.

COLONEL. Yes, yes, I know, I have no doubt. I am just saying that every man dreams of a woman like you: educated, smart and beautiful. But obviously not everyone has Youssef Wakrem's luck. I think generally your generation has better luck than ours.

SANA'A. Sorry, I don't...

COLONEL. Well, times have changed... these days men and women are free to pick their partners.

SANA'A. I see...

COLONEL. Do you mind if I light a cigar? Sorry, I'm being very informal here. Do you mind?

SANA'A. Not at all.

COLONEL. You won't think less of me? I know women these days are a bit sensitive.

SANA'A. On the contrary, we have to be flexible, always. The problem is some people build a lot of walls around themselves, with time those walls begin to restrict one's freedom. We should always be willing to build and destroy with the same gusto. With the same confidence.

COLONEL. Wow! You are truly magnificent. That's exactly what I wanted to say. Your words go straight to the heart.

SANA'A. Thank you.

COLONEL. Sorry, I didn't even ask your name.

SANA'A. Sana'a.

COLONEL. Truly honoured to meet you. Women like you are a rare breed.

SANA'A. Honestly, Colonel, I'm just like anyone else. I have my good points and my bad points.

COLONEL. Trust me, my wife and I can't even manage a ten-minute conversation, and when we talk, it's always... of no substance. Our marriage started off bland and after twenty years of marriage it's no better. A man needs a real woman by his side, someone to talk to and share dreams and ambitions with... I had to do without these things... Sorry, am I keeping you?

SANA'A. No, no, not at all, I just... had nothing to say, really.

COLONEL. You don't need to say anything, it's enough for me that you are listening. I can't seem to help myself with you...

SANA'A. We all at some point feel the need to talk to someone. A problem shared is a problem halved.

COLONEL. You really think we can do that, lessen our burden?

SANA'A. The burden will always be there. But the weight of it will lessen.

COLONEL. I really like the way you think, you make me feel like a little boy.

*SANA'A laughs.*

See what you do to me? Real men are always reduced to little boys in front of such powerful beauty.

SANA'A. You're too kind.

*Awkward moment.*

COLONEL. So, anyway, let me tell you what happened to me recently. At the end of last year I had to take the new officers to Rabat to have them sworn in. Usually there is a big party for the senior members of the army after, and everyone brings their wives. However, my wife just isn't right for these sort of events. I came up with a plan, I went to a hotel, I headed straight to the most stunning woman there, with a bit of help from a couple of beers, I started chatting to her. The beers made it seem feasible, possible. She liked the idea, became excited, and agreed... I bought her a slinky black dress. The party went fantastically.

*Starts laughing.*

Sorry, I thought you'd find my story funny... Never mind. I just wanted to hear you laugh... I didn't ask why you are here?

SANA'A. Colonel, I came to give you a package to send to Youssef in the Congo.

COLONEL. Sure, not a problem, I have a little favour to ask, though... Next week I have to attend an important party here in Meknes... Why don't you come with me?

SANA'A. Oh... Wait, are you serious? Or are you trying to make me laugh again?

COLONEL. This time, I'm serious... Of course, this will stay between us.

SANA'A. ... I'm sorry, Colonel, I can't really do that.

COLONEL. Not a problem, forget about it, what did you say was in the package?

SANA'A. Some home-made sweets and a videotape.

COLONEL. Why not send them by post?

SANA'A. I am not sure. It was Youssef's idea. Maybe because normal post doesn't reach him.

COLONEL. Yes, yes, you are right. But sending it will take time. I have to send it to Rabat. And they then send it to the Congo. What's in here again?

SANA'A. Home-made sweets and a videotape.

COLONEL. The sweets are no problem. What's on the video-tape?

SANA'A. Nothing important, just a little message to bring a smile to his face.

COLONEL. See, I was right; Lieutenant Youssef is indeed a very lucky man because he has a woman like you.

*He moves closer to her, she stands up. His body is right next to hers, she doesn't move.*

Don't worry, I will sign for the package today so it can leave for Rabat tomorrow, and if you need anything else, I am right here.

*He reaches for her neck and begins undoing the top buttons of her shirt.*

You should loosen those buttons.

*He kisses her cheek and moves even closer. She starts doing her shirt up.*

You can count on me. If you come back tomorrow I'll let you know what I can do about your package.

SANA'A. I trust you, Colonel.

SANA'A *leaves. The* COLONEL *opens the package and eats the sweets, takes the videotape, puts it in the video player and watches.*

### Scene Eight

*The African field.* YOUSSEF *pushing* JOSEPH DIWI *in a wheelchair.*

JOSEPH. Each star in the sky represents a Congolese who died in battle.

There will come a time when the nights of the Congo will be as bright as day, thanks to these stars. That time will truly come. Don't think too much. In your place all I would think about is the road that would lead me to my wife's bed. The best feeling in the world is being in a woman's arms.

YOUSSEF (*laughs*). Yeah, but you can't stay in those arms for ever…

JOSEPH. You will understand when you get to my age.

YOUSSEF. You know something? I am here for my wife.

JOSEPH (*laughs*). Your wife wants you here?

YOUSSEF *doesn't respond.*

No answer – does your wife want you here?

*Again, no answer.*

There is a lot you can do to get out of serving in this hell-hole. You can pretend to be sick, you can disobey orders. All is fair in love and war, lie or run away.

YOUSSEF. I am a coward, I can't run away, Joseph. Even if I do run away, where do I go? Just five kilometres from here fire falls like rain.

JOSEPH. There is always a solution. Listen, Youssef! You shouldn't try to convince yourself that you are here to protect democracy.

YOUSSEF. Oh, I don't believe in this false utopia, and I am no longer fooled by this uniform.

JOSEPH. Do something. Don't waste time. Here nothing is certain, save someone today and he would shoot you for a dollar tomorrow. You heard of what happened in Bunia. No one can imagine the massacre. They ruined our lives, those generals of diamonds and coltan.

Forget all that, give me a cigarette.

*They both light their cigarettes.*

We can't talk about all this without a smoke.

The war is much weaker than we believe, I'm going to tell you a story.

YOUSSEF. It seems you tell a lot of stories here in Africa.

JOSEPH. I am not a great storyteller. In Africa, when a story-teller dies, the whole tribe mourns, it's as if a library burned down.

YOUSSEF. I swear, man! You're a great storyteller. When I go back to Morocco, I'll have a lot of stories to tell.

JOSEPH. This is a story about a woman who was deaf, completely deaf. She could hear nothing. Every afternoon, she would carry her child on her back and work her huge peanut field. One afternoon, while she was there quietly working away on her field, a man approached her, a man completely deaf who was looking for his sheep. Listen well. He asked

the woman, 'Madam. I am looking for my sheep, their
tracks have led me to your field. Can you help me find
them? My sheep are easy to recognise, amongst them is a
wounded sheep. Madam, if you help me find my sheep I
will give you the wounded one.' She responded with, 'My
field stretches all the way over there.' Not understanding
him, she thought he was asking where her field ended. The
man followed the direction she indicated and as luck would
have it he found his sheep grazing peacefully behind a bush.
Happily he herded them and came to give the woman the
wounded sheep as he promised, but she didn't understand,
unable to hear anything, she thought the man was accusing
her of wounding his sheep, so she became angry: 'Mister, I
did not wound your sheep, go accuse someone else but
leave me alone, I have never laid eyes on your sheep.' When
he saw that she was angry, he assumed that she didn't want
this wounded sheep but preferred another bigger, healthier
one, so in turn he became angry. 'Madam, it was this sheep
that I promised you, there is no way I am going to give you
one of my big sheep,' so they were both angry and the only
solution was to go in front of a tribunal in the Africa of old.
This took place in the village under the shade of a large tree
where meetings between officials often took place... In the
presence of the judge who was the village chief, and all the
village nobles, the man and woman both stood to present
their quarrel. After greeting everyone, the woman stated her
case. 'This man found me in my field, he asked me where
my field stopped and I showed him and returned to my
work. He disappeared for a while and returned with some
sheep and accused me of wounding one of them. I swear,
your honour, I had never seen those sheep before in my life,
and this is the reason we come before you today.' Now it
was the man's turn to present his case. 'Your honour, I was
looking for my sheep, and their tracks led me to this
woman's field. I promised if she helped me find them I
would give her one of them, and I specifically offered her
the wounded one. She showed me where they were, and in
return I gave her the sheep I promised. But she became

angry and demanded I give her one of the larger sheep. Your honour, do you think I should give her the larger one?' The judge stood up, he was as deaf as a post. He noticed the child on the woman's back and he assumed this was a small domestic argument, so he addressed the man. 'Sir, this child is so obviously your son. He is a mini-you, I think you are an awful husband, and you, madam, have you no shame? Must you hang your dirty laundry for the whole world to see? You can sort these matters quietly yourself, go back home, I have no doubt you will reconcile.' After hearing the judge's verdict, everyone fell about laughing, and their laughter infected the judge, the man and the woman, they all laughed until they had tears in their eyes, all they could do was laugh since they understood nothing.

YOUSSEF *laughs*.

Is there something in this story that makes you laugh?

YOUSSEF. Maybe we laugh so we don't cry.

JOSEPH. Did you enjoy the story?

YOUSSEF. It was great... I'm going to bed... Shall I take you back?

JOSEPH. No... I want to stay and stare at the stars.

YOUSSEF. Take care. See you tomorrow.

JOSEPH. Reflect on what I said to you.

**Scene Nine**

*The flat.* YOUSSEF *is sitting in a wheelchair by the window, smoking,* SANA'A *enters from outside.*

SANA'A (*kisses him*). Don't worry, I'm not gonna stop you smoking.

YOUSSEF (*putting the cigarette out angrily*). Stop it, stop treating me like a baby.

SANA'A. Is my baby too big for this?

*She pinches his nose.*

Come on… smile.

YOUSSEF. Sorry… When I have the bandages changed, my legs start to burn again.

SANA'A. Don't worry, soon the burning will stop. Do you want a coffee?

YOUSSEF. I drank too much already.

SANA'A. How about something to eat?

YOUSSEF. Not hungry.

SANA'A (*going out on the balcony*). The weather is lovely, come see…

YOUSSEF (*gets closer*). Sorry, can't take you out.

SANA'A. I am happy to see the world with you from right here.

YOUSSEF (*taking a letter out of his shirt pocket*). This arrived from Rabat.

SANA'A (*reads it*). That's great.

YOUSSEF. No, it isn't.

SANA'A. Why do you say that?

YOUSSEF. I'm not going.

SANA'A. How long are you going to hide for?

YOUSSEF. I am not a criminal who needs to hide, not someone skiving off work. I told you I don't want to see anyone, I don't want anyone to greet me. I don't want anyone taking my picture while I am slipping and sliding from this pram, I don't want that music to ring in my ears, I don't want to say the things they are waiting for me to say. I can't stand reaching out for that envelope that contains the price of my legs.

SANA'A. You have to go, this is in honour of you and everyone who spilled their blood in the Congo. If you don't go then they would have screwed you twice. You lost your legs doing your job. The people who are responsible need to see that. Take that envelope with pride with your head held up high, let those bastards who push you to the front and hide behind you be ashamed of touching these envelopes with their filthy hands. Tell it exactly as it is.

YOUSSEF. I don't have the energy for all that.

I lost all my strength when my legs went flying up in front of me, all I see in front of me is bone and meat being sawn off, all I hear is the sound of bullets, alarms, trucks pulling up full of petrified people, that liar the Colonel, I still see Hamid Bouzidi's guts spilled out in front of me.

SANA'A. It's time for your medicine.

*She hands it to him.* YOUSSEF *throws the pills onto the floor.*

You need to take it.

YOUSSEF. Why?

Is it going to bring my legs back?

Is it going to let me make love to you?

Is it going to give us a Maisa or a Mahdy?

No, no, and a big fat NO.

SANA'A (*picking up the pills*). Enough, enough... Calm down, this is Allah's will.

YOUSSEF. Allah didn't do this, I did this! I went looking for the villa and the car and the bank account, I listened to the people until they pissed on me...

SANA'A. We have to let all this go, we'll start again, that's all...

YOUSSEF. Easier said than done.

SANA'A. You know we can adopt...

YOUSSEF. You need to leave me.

SANA'A. Oh, for God's sake, stop this. This is my home.

YOUSSEF. Please, just leave me. You're a beautiful woman with a big heart, you need a man to take you by the hand and show you the world, not eighty kilograms of meat plunked on a wheelchair.

SANA'A. You need to stay positive, that's the man I know, no matter what.

Why don't I pack your suitcase and we can go to the seaside? This time of year it'll be empty, we can smell the sea, sit in the coffee shop and watch the sunset. We can sleep when we want, wake when we want, we can taste pure laziness and really relax, eat breakfast at midday, eat fish while it's still fluttering, sit on rocks at night and watch the lights of the fishing boats...

YOUSSEF. The sea and train aren't for me any more. Look at me! Can I wear shorts? Or even get on the train without help...?

I need to be a bit more practical, maybe find a small ground-floor flat, I need to get used to this chair.

SANA'A. You're already talking about yourself as if you are alone.

YOUSSEF. What will you stay for? Trust me, your mum will be over the moon when you go back.

SANA'A. You forgot I left her to be with you.

YOUSSEF. No, I didn't.

SANA'A. Well then?

   Look, take your medicine and forget all this rubbish.

YOUSSEF. These pills are bitter, I need to ask the doctor to change them.

SANA'A. All medicine is bitter.

YOUSSEF. Maybe that's why it's medicine.

SANA'A. I'll go get the bed ready.

YOUSSEF. Sana'a, there's something I need to tell you.

SANA'A. Don't you think you told me enough today?

YOUSSEF. Last thing, you need to know this, I've put it off long enough. I've been thinking about telling you since I got back…

SANA'A. This sounds exciting, okay, go ahead, shoot.

YOUSSEF. I slept with someone in the Congo.

SANA'A. What do you mean, you slept with someone?

YOUSSEF. What do you think I mean?

SANA'A. What? Just like that?

YOUSSEF. It was out of my hands.

SANA'A. Out of your hands? Did she force you to drop your trousers at gunpoint?

YOUSSEF. I tried to stay away from her, I don't know how it happened.

SANA'A. Shut up, stop talking, stop rubbing it in.

YOUSSEF. That's why I keep telling you to leave. The Youssef you know is not the one sitting in front of you.

Maybe I deserve all this.

My legs flew off a week after I slept with Shandourai.

SANA'A. Stop talking…

YOUSSEF. Maybe your mum was right after all.

SANA'A. You are all the same, they don't give you that uniform until they kill your souls.

*SANA'A runs into one of the rooms and slams the door shut.*

YOUSSEF (*going to the door*). It wasn't because I fancied her… I don't know, maybe she reminded me of you, or maybe I felt sorry for her. She was scared… Shit, we were all scared. It could even be all that stuff Hamid Bouzidi was saying… Whatever it was, the only thing that has any meaning in my life is you.

*He lights a cigarette.*

*Silence.*

*SANA'A comes out looking like she has been crying.*

SANA'A. Stop smoking!

*She takes the cigarette and puts it out in the ashtray.*

Time for bed.

*She pushes the wheelchair inside the bedroom.*

*The End.*

# THE HOUSE

البيت

ARZÉ KHODR

*translated by*

KHALID LAITH

**Arzé Khodr**

Arzé Khodr was born in Beirut, Lebanon, in 1976 just a year after the beginning of the civil war. She graduated in Theatre Studies in 1999 and has worked as a theatre teacher. She is also an actress and has taken part in many short films. She works as a writer for television.

**Khalid Laith**

Originally from the island of Bahrain in the Persian Gulf, Khalid Laith grew up and was educated between the Middle East, the UK and the United States. He trained as an actor at the Central School of Speech and Drama in London, where he currently lives. Next to his acting work, Khalid works as a translator in various fields, he edits short films and documentaries, and composes and produces his own music.

*The House* was first performed as a rehearsed reading as part of the *I Come From There: New Plays from the Arab World* season in the Jerwood Theatre Upstairs, Royal Court Theatre, London, on 15 November 2008, with the following cast:

| | |
|---|---|
| NADIA | Thusitha Jayasundera |
| REEM | Nathalie Armin |
| NABEEL | Ray Panthaki |
| *Director* | Maria Aberg |

The play was also read at Espace El Teatro in Tunis, Tunisia, in February 2009.

**Characters**

NADIA, *female, forties*
REEM, *female, mid-thirties*
NABEEL, *male, early thirties*

**Notes and references**

*Wallah* – 'by Allah'
*W'hyat Allah* – for God's sake, or 'on Allah's life', a Lebanese
    expression
*Ya Allah* – 'my dear God'
*Yalla* – 'hurry up' or 'come on'
*Ya'ni* – 'you mean' (can also mean 'I mean', 'meaning', 'sort
    of', see notes for *Egyptian Products*)


Mentioned by Nabeel on page 148, Solidere s.a.l. is a Lebanese
joint-stock company in charge of planning and redeveloping
Beirut Central District following the conclusion of the country's
devastating civil war in 1990. By agreement with the government, Solidere enjoys special powers of eminent domain as well
as a limited regulatory authority codified in law, making the
company a unique form of public-private partnership.

## ACT ONE

### Scene One

*A living room in an old Beirut home.* REEM *is sitting.* NADIA *comes through the kitchen door. They are both dressed in black.*

NADIA. I finished cleaning the kitchen. What a day it's been, I've been on my feet since seven this morning!

REEM. You're a masochist, you enjoy the exhaustion...

NADIA. What do you want us to do? Leave Mama without a forty-day memorial?

REEM. We could've just had something intimate, without the extended family. A simple lunch. I don't think there's anyone we know who didn't come by today.

NADIA. So, let them come...

REEM. I just want what's best for you! You've worn yourself out!

NADIA. It's nothing.

REEM. Fine, it's nothing.

NADIA. Did you see Nabeel's wife? A layer of foundation on her face this thick... (*Indicates a thickness of five centimetres with her fingers.*)

REEM. You know her. Full make-up no matter what the occasion.

NADIA. I can't stand the woman. How can Nabeel be happy with her?

REEM. He seems happy...

NADIA. Happy, living under her thumb...

REEM. Oh, let them be. Sit down, I want to talk to you.

NADIA, *very carefully, sits down.*

NADIA. I know…

REEM. What?

NADIA. You want to leave…

REEM. Yes. I think it's time. I have to get back home.

NADIA. This is your home.

REEM. Nadia, do me a favour –

NADIA. What about you doing me a favour? You know I can't live alone.

REEM. Why can't you? You'd be better off!

NADIA. No, I wouldn't. Reem, please don't leave so soon after Mama's death.

REEM. Nadia, I've been here for forty days. Longer, two months in fact, ever since Mama went to hospital.

NADIA. Two months. Seems like only yesterday. I can't believe it, she was fine… and in a blink she got a fever, then she's gone… (*Starts to cry.*)

REEM. I know. Every time the phone rings, I expect it to be her. I catch myself saying, 'What does that woman want now…!' How life unfolds…

*Silence.*

You know that in a month or so I'm going to Qatar, right?

NADIA. Yes.

REEM. I'm signing a six-month contract…

NADIA. You told me.

REEM. And my contract might get extended, I'll be away for quite a while.

NADIA. I know!

REEM. So whichever way, I won't be able to live with you.

NADIA. You could stay until it's time for you to travel.

REEM. I don't want to. I want to go home. I want to leave. I can't stand it here.

NADIA. Ah well, you could have said that earlier. It's nice to know you hate my company. Admit it!

REEM. For God's sake, I didn't say that.

NADIA. Just for a few more days...

REEM. Nadia. Nadia, why are you doing this? It's been ten years since I left this house, and I'm always hearing the same thing. Not once did Mama call me without asking when I'd be coming back, when I'd be sleeping here in this house again...

NADIA. Well, she's dead now. What else do you want?

REEM. What else do I want? You think I wanted her to die? You think I'm happy now?

NADIA. I didn't mean to...

REEM. No, go on, say it. *W'hyat Allah...* Enough. Listen to me, Nadia, I have to go back to my house, I need to prepare for my trip and organise my life. I'm leaving you tomorrow.

NADIA. No, Reem, please. I can't, I just can't stay in this house alone.

REEM. We've been over this already, eventually I'll have to leave. You'll go back to work at some point...

NADIA. You expect me to sleep here on my own.

REEM. And? I sleep on my own.

NADIA. I just can't!

REEM. Well then, get the neighbours' daughter, that girl Nina, to sleep over.

NADIA. Really?! And what am I supposed to say to her? 'Pack your things, you're moving in with me?'

REEM. What do you expect from me? Hire a maid if you need the company.

NADIA. I don't see why you want to live alone when we have this big empty house. What's wrong about living together?

REEM. I don't want us to live together.

NADIA. Mama's gone now, and I certainly won't get in your way.

REEM. Enough, Nadia. I've got a million things to take care of. I need to go back home tomorrow.

NADIA. Oh, I get it. You have a boyfriend you don't want to bring back here. That must be it.

REEM. Whether or not I have a boyfriend is simply none of your business.

NADIA. So, it's definitely that. Why else would you have left ten years ago? Except to go and sleep with your Shi'ite boyfriend.

REEM. Ah, so that's what this is about. God forbid I'm sleeping with someone, God forbid a man even touches me. Of course, I'm living alone because I want to be free enough to slut about. Is that what you think of me? I left ten years ago because I'm a whore, not because I couldn't stand the life I had in this place. No, I 'ran away' – as if I was fifteen when I left, not twenty-six. And I'll have you know that when I left, I did sleep with my Shi'ite boyfriend, whenever and however I wanted.

NADIA. I don't want to know any more.

REEM. Of course you want to know. You want to know if I'm sleeping with someone. You can relax, I'm not. And if I want to go home, it's not so I can get fucked whenever I want it. I want some room to breathe and feel alive again, because this place is killing me.

*There's a knock at the door.*

NADIA. Someone's at the door, I hope they didn't hear you.

REEM. Let them hear. I couldn't care less.

NADIA *opens the door.* NABEEL *enters.*

NABEEL. I came back, thought I'd check on you, see if you needed anything. (*To* NADIA.) You all right? You look tired.

NADIA. It's been an exhausting day.

REEM. I told her we didn't need such a big event.

NADIA. Oh, shut up, you… trollop.

NABEEL. What's wrong? Have you two been fighting?

REEM. Oh, it's nothing. I'm a slut and Nadia can't live on her own, that's all.

NADIA. I don't want you staying here any more. Go to your own house.

REEM. You sure?

NADIA. I'm sure. There's no living with people like you, anyway.

REEM. God forbid you should live with people like me. Careful you don't stoop to my level.

NABEEL. Just calm down a minute. What happened exactly?

NADIA. I was just asking her to stay with me a little bit longer. I can't be in this house alone. You know me, Nabeel. I can't sleep alone, I stay awake all night.

NABEEL. I know.

NADIA. But she wants to leave because she has more important things to tend to.

REEM. Of course I want to leave. I have to leave. I've got to be in Qatar in six weeks, Nabeel.

NABEEL. Just stay here for these six weeks, and then Allah will sort it out.

REEM. How's he supposed to do that? Now or later, it's all the same.

NADIA. She doesn't have to stay if she doesn't want to. Just leave, I'll be fine.

NABEEL. Reem, can't you stay a few more days? What's the worst that can happen? You'll be in another country soon enough.

REEM. I've got so much to take care of before I leave…

NABEEL. Well then, take care of it during the day and sleep here at night. That's not too difficult, is it? (*Light-heartedly.*) And you, Nadia, stop torturing your little sister.

NADIA. Me, torture her? She'd put Guantanamo to shame!

NABEEL. I know. *Wallah* I know.

REEM. *Wallah* what? You too, Nabeel?!

NABEEL. Just relax, Reem. You were away for so long… you never called. You should soften a little, Mama's only been dead forty days. Nothing will happen to you if you stay with Nadia a little longer.

NADIA. Listen to me, Reem, you know I want you stay with me with all my heart, but you do whatever you want.

**Scene Two**

*Inside the house.* NADIA *is standing on a chair in front of a large cabinet, polishing the silverware. There's a knock at the door.*

NADIA. Just a second.

*She gets down.*

REEM (*on the other side of the door*). It's me… Never mind, I found the key.

NADIA *gets to the door just as* REEM *opens it.*

Hi.

NADIA. Hi.

*She helps* REEM *carry some bags in.*

REEM. No, it's all right, I'll take them up to the room in a sec.

NADIA. No problem, we'll do it together.

NADIA *heads for the stairs carrying a heavy load.*

REEM (*sharply*). I said I'll take them up myself!

NADIA. Okay, fine. I won't help you... if you don't want my help.

REEM *carries the bags up the stairs, into the room. She comes back out again.*

REEM. Anything left downstairs?

NADIA (*looking around*). No.

REEM *comes down and checks outside the front door.*

REEM. *Ya Allah!* I must've forgotten them by the bed!

NADIA. What is it?

REEM. My cream-coloured shoes. I went all the way back to my house just to get them. I wanted to wear them tonight. I got everything except for the shoes.

NADIA. Tonight? Are you going out?

REEM. Yes, in an hour or so. I've had enough, *w'hyat Allah* I'm sick of moving!

NADIA (*putting the chair she was standing on away*). Do you want to have a bite to eat before you go?

REEM. What have we got?

NADIA. There's salad in the fridge, and you've got some steaks...

REEM. No, no, I'll have dinner with my friends. (*To herself.*) What am I going to do about the shoes?

NADIA. Wear something else.

REEM. I can't keep track of what clothes I've got here and what I've left at my place.

NADIA. I told you we should have just moved everything here. You'll be leaving that house eventually. Right?

REEM. I don't know, Nadia. I just don't know.

NADIA. What do you mean? Aren't you off to Qatar? You don't want to be paying rent on an empty house.

REEM. I paid in advance. Four months still left on the lease.

NADIA. I don't believe you! You want to pay for a house in Beirut while living in Qatar.

REEM. I was thinking of just letting the lease run out. I'll know if the Qatar contract will be renewed. I could always get in touch with the landlord if I needed to come back.

NADIA. I see.

REEM. What's that supposed to mean?

NADIA. You can do whatever you like. I'm not getting involved!

REEM. Oh, you're right, you're not involved at all. It's not like I've been moving my things every day, running between two houses, not knowing where I am, just to make you happy.

NADIA. Please don't go out of your way to do me any favours. What have I done to you? Don't you have a good life here? You don't have to answer to anyone. I even wash and iron your clothes…

REEM. No one asked you to wash or iron anything.

NADIA. It's all right. You don't owe me for it.

REEM. Of course, you're the good one and I'm the trollop.

NADIA. I didn't say that.

REEM. Oh yes, I'm the heartless bitch who left this house. I was the problem child. I had a Shi'ite boyfriend. I don't care about anyone. I suppose I killed Baba too!

NADIA. That's enough, no one said that!

REEM. You think it all the time. I know Mama felt the same.

NADIA. No, she didn't. You blame her for everything.

REEM. I did blame her for everything, eventually. She started
it. She once said to me, 'Your father might still be alive if it
weren't for you.' Who says that to an eight-year-old child?

NADIA. She didn't mean it… She was devastated.

REEM. She meant every word. She mourned him for the rest of
her life, but they were never a normal, happy couple. She
made his life miserable, never mind what she did to us. She
only got worse after he died.

NADIA. Don't be so cold-hearted.

REEM. Well, I am. I only wish I was like this a long time ago.
It would've made things easier today.

NADIA. Well… All this because of your shoes?

REEM. Oh, I wish… If only your life were solely determined
by your shoes!

NADIA. No need to get upset before you go out now. I've got a
pair of cream-coloured shoes upstairs. Try them on.

REEM. We're not the same size.

NADIA. Try them. Maybe with a pair of thick socks…

REEM. I don't think they'll fit, Nadia. It won't work. I'll just
wear something else.

## Scene Three

*The house is empty. There's a knock at the door. REEM comes down the stairs. She looks through the spyhole then opens the door.*

REEM. Don't you have a key?

NABEEL. I do, but I don't know where it is. Is Nadia gone?

REEM. Just left for work. Want some coffee?

NABEEL. No, *merci*. I had one at home.

REEM. Well, sit down, I need to talk to you.

NABEEL. As long as it's quick, I've got an appointment at nine.

REEM. Oh, Nabeel, you're always rushing off. Didn't I ask you yesterday to give me half an hour of your time?!

NABEEL. Fine, I'm sitting. What's up? Still fighting with Nadia?

REEM. Yes… Well, no… Poor thing, she's doing her best not to disturb me, so I don't pack up and leave… but I'm suffocating, I can't stand it…

NABEEL. It's all right. How long till Qatar? A month and you're free, not long to go. I'd ask her to stay at mine, but you know what she's like with my wife, and I'm not brave enough to mention it.

REEM. I don't expect you to do that. That's not what I'm talking about. If I stay here then, when I come back, where do I come back to?

NABEEL. What?

REEM. Where do I go when I come back from Qatar? Where will home be?

NABEEL. 'Where will home be?' What do you mean?

REEM. Don't play dumb, Nabeel. I'll be in Qatar for at least six months. My lease ends in four. I either pay rent on an empty house, or move all my things into this one.

NABEEL. Move your things and just come back here when you're done. Isn't that cheaper for you?

REEM. Nabeel, my dear brother, concentrate with me here – I just told you I can't stand living here! If I move out of my place completely, I'll have to stay here for good!

NABEEL. Not necessarily. Just move your things in here. When you get back, rent your old place again. It isn't that complicated.

REEM. It is complicated. Haven't you heard Nadia? 'I can't live alone, don't leave I won't be in your way, what do you want to eat, what do you want to drink...' You think she'd let me leave that easily?

NABEEL. She'll get used to living alone while you're away.

REEM. She'll be forced to live alone while I'm gone... and when I get back, she'll force me into staying.

NABEEL. Reem, honestly. We'll cross that bridge when we come to it. Besides, no one's been able to force you into any-thing. You are always so stubborn.

REEM. It's different now. Nadia's been laying on the guilt, thick. Every time I come back here, I decide to speak to her about leaving, but she won't let me. She's smothering me with questions, asking if I'm hungry or thirsty, if I need to rest... I'm only alone when she's crying in Mama's room. Honestly, it's driving me mad. I feel as though I'll be trapped here for ever.

NABEEL. 'Trapped here for ever'?

REEM. Yes, trapped. Forced to live in this house with Nadia for the rest of my days.

NABEEL. And... what's wrong with that?

REEM. What do you mean? 'What's wrong with that?' I'd go numb, go crazy, I'd die...

NABEEL. Enough already! What do you want?

REEM. I want to sell the house.

NABEEL. What?

REEM. Sell the house and split the money. That way I can buy my own place, Nadia can have her own place too, and we'll get her a housekeeper to stay with her so she doesn't feel so alone. You can do what you like with your share.

NABEEL. Oh God!

REEM. It's the best option.

NABEEL. How can you even be thinking about this?

REEM. Are you telling me it's never crossed your mind?

NABEEL. No, honestly, it hasn't.

REEM. Well, now you can think about it. It's a big house, in the centre of Beirut. You know that property prices have been rising... I had the house valued recently, we could get two and half million dollars for it. That means eight hundred thousand each. Have you bought your house yet?

NABEEL. Still paying the bank mortgage.

REEM. Perfect. You can pay that off.

NABEEL. Yes, but...

REEM. But what?

NABEEL. I don't know, I'm a little shocked. Are you serious about this?

REEM. Yes, Nabeel, to my own house.

NABEEL. Have you mentioned this to Nadia?

REEM. Not yet, I'm running it by you first. What do you think?

NABEEL. To be honest, it's never crossed my mind. It is a big house, and of course we'd get a good deal of money for it, but I've never thought of it, especially with both of you living here.

REEM. I am not living here, and I don't want to be. That's why we have to sell it.

NABEEL. Truthfully, do you need the money? Do you have debts or a bank loan you need to –

REEM. No, *Wallah*, no. I just think that selling the house would be better for us, and for the house! It needs a lot of work done... repainting, the plumbing, the roof leaks, and someone should bring the garden back to life. I'm going away soon. Do you really think Nadia can handle all that on her own? She could use the money, you know, and you don't need that mortgage hanging over your head.

NABEEL. It's a fair point. I'm with you. But we'd be selling our parents' house, the house we grew up in...

REEM. Yes, I realise that. The whole point is to sell the house we grew up in.

NABEEL. Always the troublemaker, Reem!

REEM. How dare you?! Two months I've been eating shit and shutting up, when you know damn well how much I hate being here. So selling the house and getting a place of my own makes me a troublemaker? You call making good use of our only inheritance 'trouble'? All I want for us is to live comfortably.

NABEEL. That's all you care about, living comfortably, every-thing else can go to hell. Do you know what selling this house would really mean? Have you considered Nadia at all? Imagine the consequences...

REEM. I've thought this through, and know very well Nadia won't accept it initially, that's why I spoke to you first, so we can convince her together.

NABEEL. Bravo, Reem, scheming against your sister. Making trouble to get your own way.

REEM. You seemed to like the idea...

NABEEL. Don't you understand that all my life I've tried to stay out of your problems? I left this house too, you know. You're not the only one who had a hard time here. Of course I like the idea, why shouldn't I? But do you know what it's going to cost? Can you imagine the headaches? You don't see a problem with it because you create the problem in the first place, and if a person chooses to ignore you, you insist on making their life a misery just to please yourself. I can't deal with it any more, Reem. I've always tried to balance things out, but I've had it up to here with these female hysterics. I want to live comfortably too. I'd sooner see the back of this place, believe me, but this idea of yours could stir up endless trouble, and who'll be in the firing line, huh? Me. Who has to mediate between you two? Both of you have always been like this and I accept it. 'They're my sisters. I'm their only brother...' But now you want to start a war and you want me to be on your side?

REEM. No, Nabeel, no. Do me a favour and listen to me. I'm not trying to manipulate you, or trying to cause trouble, *Wallah*, believe me. I just can't stand the idea of living here, you know. I want something good to come out of this house for once, instead of the misery it's given us.

NABEEL. Oh, of course, this plan sounds misery-proof!

REEM. Look, if we sell, at least we'd have some money to spend for once. You do have a point, I know it could be difficult at first, but just think of getting rid of this place for good. The thought of this house not existing any more makes me so happy...

NABEEL. You should listen to yourself. You're sounding a little crazy...

REEM. No I'm not, I've never been saner. I've done my research. Did you know that if Nadia refuses, the two of us could legally oblige her to sell her share of the house?

NABEEL. What? Take your own sister to court?

REEM. If she gave us no other choice.

NABEEL. Reem. For God's sake, give it a break! You want to fight your own sister for her share of a tattered old house, to get us involved in an ordeal with courts and lawyers? And for what? The house will be all yours in the very end. And you don't need the money at the moment, do you?

REEM. No, I don't.

NABEEL. If we're ever desperate to sell, then so be it. But do you have to cause friction between us now? Those doors are closed for a reason. Aren't you the one who moves on and never looks back? Forget about the house, let's just go on with our lives. If the house needs to be sold someday, we'll find the right time to do it.

REEM. That time has come.

NABEEL. You're adamant?

REEM. Yes.

NABEEL. Listen, I'm not getting in between you and Nadia. Don't even dream of it. But I'll tell you one thing, if both of you agree to it, we'll sell. If you don't, I won't be getting involved in your dirty games, dragging this through the courts. You hear me?

REEM. I hear you. *Ya'ni* you're a coward.

NABEEL. You can say what you like, but don't think you can manipulate me.

NABEEL *leaves*.

REEM. Of course... Only your wife can do that now...

**Scene Four**

REEM *is in the house. We hear the keys in the front door, and*
NADIA *enters.*

NADIA. What's this? You're home before me today…

REEM. I thought I'd come home early. I've boiled us some
pasta and bought tomatoes so you can make some of
'Nadia's Special Sauce'.

NADIA. 'Nadia's Special Sauce'! You still remember that?

REEM. How could I forget?! I've never had a plate of pasta
anywhere else without yours coming to mind.

NADIA. Really! You've never mentioned it.

REEM. I've always loved your cooking. You've always said I
can't cook.

NADIA. Well, you can't. What was it Mama used say? 'The
way you cook, it's a good thing you never poisoned yourself.'

REEM. She never said it to me. You'd tell me later.

NADIA. That's right.

REEM. So, how about that 'Special Sauce'?

NADIA. It's a bit of chore. I'm tired, and can't be bothered
with chopping onions and tomatoes…

REEM. Never mind. I'll juice a lemon, we can have the pasta
with that, and maybe some oil.

NADIA (*cringes at the thought of that food*). No, *yalla* I'll
make the sauce, if you're craving it. Let me rest a little first.

REEM. Don't worry about it. I'll eat anything.

NADIA. No, no. Just let me put my feet up for a bit.

REEM. It's all right, you can make it tomorrow, or for Sunday
lunch. I just wanted us to have a meal together, so we could
talk.

NADIA. Ah, so there's something to talk about.

REEM. Yes, and it's rather important.

NADIA. *Yalla*, tell me…

REEM. Nadia, I've been thinking about making our lives easier…

NADIA. In what respect?

REEM. In all respects… You come home from work tired, only to do more work at home. You do all the cooking and the cleaning. And, you know, the paint is peeling off the walls, the roof leaks, sometimes the toilets overflow. And I don't think the garden is even recognisable as a garden any more. Well, it's just that I'll be leaving soon enough, you'll be here on your own…

NADIA. What am I supposed to do?

REEM. Well… You know, houses have increased in value tremendously recently, and this big place of ours is very centrally located, it could make us some money. I was thinking about selling it and sharing the profits. We'd get, I don't know… Eight hundred thousand dollars each.

NADIA. What? You want to sell the house?

REEM. I was just thinking about it. Why not? Nabeel could pay off his mortgage. I could finally buy a house, instead of renting all my life. You could buy a house as well, and get a live-in maid… What do you think?

NADIA. Have you gone mad? Are you trying to kill me?! You want to get rid of me!

REEM. Not at all, I just want you to be comfortable.

NADIA. What do you know about my comfort?

REEM. Fine, then it's for my comfort. I want to sell the house. Do you mind?

NADIA. Yes. Of course I do. You want me to stand aside and watch you sell this house? What did this house ever do to you?

REEM. What did it do? It wore the hell out of me! I want to get rid of it and know that I never have to come back here again.

NADIA. You don't have to come back. You're free to go. No one's forcing you to stay.

REEM. Yes, Nadia, you are. Forever reminding me how you just can't live alone. Always playing the victim.

NADIA. I'll live by myself. What's it to you? You don't care about me, anyway.

REEM. Sure. You're the caring one. God forbid you should be flawed in any way.

NADIA. You expect me to be like you? Always turning your back and running.

REEM. Because I left this house to live my own life? You wanted me to stay here, endlessly bickering with you and your mother? You cut out my heart, both of you!

NADIA. I never did anything to hurt you. You left us, Mama broke down, I took care of everything all the time…

REEM. She broke down? Her whole life was a car crash. What about me? Wasn't I broken? Did anyone ever ask about me? What it felt like to see Baba lying on the kitchen floor like that? Oh, you were very good about drumming to Mama's tune. 'Your father would be alive if it weren't for you.' Yes, only a loving mother would say that to her daughter! I've played it back in my head a million times; if only I'd got up to get myself that glass of water, instead of nagging at him that I was thirsty, maybe then he'd be alive. I would have gone to the kitchen and come back, and that missile needn't have killed anyone. But that's not what happened. What am I supposed to do? I still remember feeling that wind pushing me back, then running to see what had happened. I found Baba on the floor, his face white with dust. A string of blood trickled from his head, down to his chin. I cried out to him, but he didn't answer. I was scared. I ran to my room. Then the screaming started. I hid under the bed, I knew something

bad had happened and it felt like it was my fault. We stayed
with the neighbours, and I heard their daughter say to her
cousin, 'She's here because her father died.' My father died.
You held my hand, and we watched cartoons. Holding hands.
I didn't know where Nabeel was...

NADIA. We came home to find Mama dressed in black.

REEM. It was all she wore after all.

NADIA. She wouldn't stop crying.

REEM. She couldn't stand me any more, but I didn't realise it
at the time.

NADIA. When did you?

REEM. Much later. Years later. I started to notice the way she
would speak to me. The things she said. I could see that she
didn't love me, and would sooner have me dead.

NADIA. That's not true.

REEM. It is. Always. 'Where are you going?' 'Why are you
going there?' If I wanted to see someone, 'You don't need to
see them.' If I ever bought anything for myself, it was, 'You
don't need it. You've got enough already.' Never anything
encouraging to say. I'm glad I was a good student, it's the
only thing she couldn't complain about.

NADIA. She said the same things to me.

REEM. She never let up. She suffocated me. I couldn't take it.

NADIA. Don't you think she suffocated me too?

REEM. You chose to accept it.

NADIA. Was I supposed to just leave her?

REEM. It wouldn't have killed her! All children leave at some
point.

NADIA. Once they're married.

REEM. I wasn't going to wait for marriage to save me.

NADIA. You left. I stayed. It's all the same anyhow. Look at us now, in the same place we were twenty years ago.

REEM. What do you mean?

NADIA. Just what I said. Nothing's changed, Reem.

REEM. Yes, it has. I'm not in the same place. You can't say that. I'm not like you. I don't want to be like you. I'm not staying in the house to end up like you.

NADIA. Don't be so self-important. What have you done with your life, anyway? You left, bravo, then what? Did you get married? Become rich? Have children? You're the same as when you were living here. Nothing's changed...

REEM. I'm not going to stay here to satisfy your pathetic need for the past. We're not going back there, Nadia. Never! I'm not growing old with you in this house so you can say you haven't missed out on family life.

NADIA. That's enough, Reem. Enough with your theories.

REEM. All your life you've been without a man. Why do you think that is?

NADIA. I wasn't lucky enough.

REEM. You, me, Auntie, none of us have been lucky. It was never down to luck. Mama was awful, convinced us men aren't worth it, all of them liars you can never rely on. And grandmother never even talked to her husband by the end of it. Ever wondered if we're cursed somehow? You know? I used to think I was born with something missing, that thing that could make men love me. I was sure that all the other girls had it, but I didn't. I was sure of it. Then I realised that I was pushing them away, all the men who could possibly love me. I wouldn't let them get close, I was sure they would only make me miserable. If Baba were alive today maybe things would be different. I don't know... maybe we would've found men useful had he been around longer. I've had enough of it, Nadia. This house...

NADIA. Leave, then. I'll live alone. Pack your things and go now, if you like.

REEM. No.

NADIA. I'm telling you, go. You're tired of this, I've certainly had enough. I'd rather be alone than have to listen to you. You're killing me, Reem. Go back to your own house… Honestly, I won't stop you any more.

REEM. No, we have to sell this house. I need a place of my own, and you need one too.

NADIA. I'm happy here. You go back to your place. Enough.

REEM. I said, no. We have to get rid of this house, someone else can live in it. I never want to set foot in this place again. You need to leave too. Why can't you understand that? You have to leave as well.

NADIA. That's enough, Reem. Calm down. Go upstairs and go to sleep. You can move your things out in the morning and leave.

REEM. Oh, I'm leaving, Nadia, and this house will be sold.

**Scene Five**

NADIA *and* NABEEL *are sitting at home*.

NADIA. You've made it clear to her that I won't be selling?

NABEEL. Yes, *wallah* I explained it to her. Why won't you believe me?

NADIA. What else does she want from us? Can't she just leave us in peace?

NABEEL. I don't know, Nadia.

NADIA. I thought she was joking at first. Thought she'd go back to hers, calm down, and just forget all about it.

NABEEL. She's not capable of forgetting. Never lets you forget it either.

NADIA. Nabeel, please, stay true to your word, don't let her have her own way. You know how much I'm attached to this house…

*We hear the keys in the door.* REEM *opens the door and enters.*

REEM. *Bonsoir.*

NADIA (*frosty*). If it isn't Madame Reem!

REEM. What? You're still on your high horse?! Can't we at least discuss this like civilised people?

NADIA. There's nothing for us to discuss. You know I don't want to sell the house.

REEM. This isn't just your house, you know.

NADIA. It is. I'm the one who lives in it.

REEM. You live in it, but the three of us own it.

NADIA. Nabeel and I aren't selling. It's two against one.

REEM. Are you sure about that? So, Nabeel? I thought you liked the idea?

NADIA. What?

NABEEL. I never said I liked it, outright. I said we'd sell, only if both of you agreed…

REEM. Your wife seems to like the idea too… very much so…

NADIA. Your wife knows about this?

NABEEL. Reem spoke to her. But it doesn't change anything. Like I said, we don't do anything until both of you agree to it.

NADIA. You've enlisted your sister-in-law? You want a war?

REEM (*patronisingly*). I really don't understand you, Nadia. This is a lucrative opportunity. You can finally be comfortable and independent.

NADIA. I am comfortable and independent.

REEM. Well, I'm not comfortable.

NADIA. That's your problem.

REEM. Yours too. I'm entitled to a third of this house and I want to sell it. It's not yours alone.

NADIA. Have I ever said otherwise? Or stopped you from coming here?

REEM. I don't want to come here. I want to sell it and finally get rid of it.

NADIA. Are you hearing this, Nabeel?

NABEEL. Could both of you please calm down so we can talk about this?

REEM. I'm as calm as can be. Nothing's the matter.

NADIA. You're right, nothing is the matter. I'm living in this house and nobody's selling it any time soon…

REEM. The three of us have inherited this house, Nadia, my dear. We all have a right to it. Nabeel?

NABEEL. Just a second here, one second. We already spoke about this, Reem, we agreed that selling the house can wait.

REEM. It can't wait!

NABEEL. You don't need the money.

REEM. No, I don't.

NADIA. Well, that's wonderful. You just want to sell the house on a whim!

REEM. Exactly! I want to sell this place because I can't stand it, I can't tolerate its stench. I can't stand these walls and everything they contain! I hate that I was ever conceived in this house, the fact that I grew up in it, and the fact that I'm standing in it now talking about it. I've never liked this house or the life I had here. I almost didn't believe it when I was finally able to afford to move out, and not have to listen to your voices again. I've never been happy in this house. Not one minute of normality. It makes me sick. I can't breathe here. They could tear this place down, for all I care. I hope it burns down. All of it, with every last thing in it.

NADIA. What is this madness?! You're crazy! You've lost your mind!

REEM. You're the one living in a silly dream. Are you really happy? You've convinced yourself that you're living like a queen in your parents' house. How stupid can you be? And you want me to live with you like this? Do you think anyone can bear living with you? Just like your mother!

NABEEL. I've had enough of both of you! I don't have to listen to this. I'm going.

NADIA. No, stay. You stay and she can go. Insulting me in my own house!

REEM (*calm*). I'm staying right here. This is my house too and I have the right to be here.

REEM *sits on a chair at the dinner table. Some time passes in complete silence.* NABEEL *sits at the other end of the table. He finds some old photo albums next to him. He opens one and finds a photo of the two sisters standing in front of their late father's car.*

NABEEL. What are these?

NADIA. The room upstairs had a leak, I thought I'd bring some things down here to keep dry, and I found those photo albums.

NABEEL. I don't remember this. When was this taken?

REEM (*moves in closer to inspect the photo*). Show me? Ah, that's the day Baba bought the Fiat. We went for a spin in it.

NABEEL. Where was I?

NADIA. At home. Where else, Nabeel? You were only six months old.

NABEEL *and* REEM *continue to flip through the photos.*

NABEEL. I'm not in a single one of these. It's just you and her.

NADIA. They're very old.

REEM. We made you a new album once you were born, we put all your photos in there. (*To* NADIA.) He was a very spoiled boy.

NABEEL. That's not true. (*To* NADIA.) You were the spoiled one.

REEM. He does have a point!

NADIA. That didn't really matter.

NABEEL. Probably not to you…

REEM. You should talk about being spoiled, the only boy after two girls…

NABEEL. But I used to feel so separate from you girls.

REEM. We were all lonely, Nabeel. I felt like I was living on another planet.

NADIA. You? Of course!

REEM. Oh, shut up!

NABEEL. I used to think you loved each other more than you loved me.

NADIA. Seriously?

NABEEL. You walked to school together, wore the same clothes, played together…

REEM. Mostly bickering and hair-pulling.

NADIA. You were always the jealous one.

REEM. No, no, no… We used to fight because you never had a sense of humour. Still don't…

NADIA. Admit that you were jealous of me!

*They both laugh.*

REEM. Even if I was jealous, that was long ago. I grew up and realised I am much prettier.

NADIA. No, no, no... That is not true.

NABEEL. You girls are unbelievable... You really are like children, weren't you fighting a minute ago?

REEM. Thanks for reminding us. So, how 'bout it, Nadia?

NADIA. I've already told you. No means no.

REEM. What do you have to say about it, Nabeel?

NABEEL. I told you both, if you two can agree on selling then we'll sell. If you can't, then no.

REEM. Yes, but what would you prefer?

NABEEL. *Ya'ni*, whatever you two want...

REEM. I want to sell...

NADIA. And I won't sell.

NABEEL. Here we go again... Don't get me involved in this. I'm not making the decision for you.

REEM. You've never made a decision in your life...

NADIA. Oh yes, just let Reem walk all over you. Typical.

NABEEL. What is wrong with you two? Fighting with each other isn't enough, so you gang up on me?

REEM. Forget it, Nabeel. Just go. You're absolutely useless.

NABEEL. Oh, I'm gone.

*He takes his jacket and leaves, closing the door behind him. The two women sit in silence.*

REEM. I'm leaving too.

NADIA. Go, good riddance. And get the idea of selling this house out of your head.

**Scene Six**

NADIA *stands outside the front gate. The gate is locked. She is looking at a piece of paper hanging on it.* NABEEL *arrives.*

NABEEL. What now?

NADIA. Have a look. Be my guest.

NABEEL. What?

NADIA. Read.

NABEEL *reads the paper, which is stamped with a red wax seal.*

NABEEL. 'This property is hereby ceased, by order of the Court of Expedited Cases in Beirut, until the closure of the case. Reem Khoury vs. Nabeel and Nadia Khoury.' So, Reem actually went through with it...

NADIA. Did you know she was going to do this?

NABEEL. Nadia, how can you ask me that?

NADIA. Well, she said you liked the idea... so does your wife. She spoke to you first about selling the house. She tells you everything...

NABEEL. You really believe I'd take you to court over this? Are you crazy? She's filed the case against me too. Don't you see my name next to yours?

NADIA. This is too much... How did we even get to this point? Where did all this come from? I don't understand why Reem is doing this...

NABEEL. Did you call the lawyer?

NADIA. I was on the phone to him for the past hour...

NABEEL. And?

NADIA. He says it's a scare tactic. 'Expedited Cases', meaning she spun this web of lies and got some hack judge to sign off on the closure, we can get it overturned easily enough...

NABEEL. Are you sure?

NADIA. That's what he says.

NABEEL. Fine, if it's only a matter of days, then we can handle it...

NADIA. How can we handle it, Nabeel? Where am I supposed to go now? Can you believe this?! I come back from work to find my own house off-limits. If it's come to this, then there's no stopping Reem at all...

NABEEL. Relax. Let's go to my house and we can talk about this.

NADIA. I don't want to relax. I want to go home...

NABEEL. Well, Nadia, have you thought about this idea of selling? Eight hundred thousand dollars would buy you nice little flat in town...

NADIA. What?! There might have been a chance of me considering it before, but after what I've seen today, not even Allah can change my mind... I know you like the idea of selling, I know... Your wife too. She's a crafty one, that Reem, she knows how to get what she wants.

NABEEL. I told you, I'd never stand with her against you. Don't you believe me? What else do you want from me? Do I need to put it in writing? I'm sick of this! I don't blame Reem for wanting to get rid of this place...

NADIA. So, it's come to this? You want to kick me out too? I don't believe this!

NABEEL. Calm down and listen to me, Nadia. I would never force you out of this house. Never. You have to believe me. Is that clear enough?

NADIA. Yes.

NABEEL. Let's head to mine, you can stay with us until we get this sorted.

NADIA. I'm not going to change my mind, Nabeel. Don't you ever ask me to think about it again...

**Scene Seven**

*Inside the house,* NADIA *is busy cleaning. There's a knock at the door, then* REEM *uses her key and enters.*

REEM. Welcome back!

NADIA. What are you doing here?

REEM. I'm paying you a nice visit. I've come to see how you are, what you're up to... I'm flying out after tomorrow.

NADIA. Great! It'll be nice to see the back of you!

REEM. Come on, Nadia! Is this how sisters speak?

NADIA. You made up all those lies. You waited for me to go to work so you can have the house sealed off. Was that very sisterly? With red wax, no less!

REEM. You're back now. Don't make such a big deal out of it.

NADIA. How dare you, Reem...? You have your own sister thrown out of her parents' house, and that's not such a big deal?!

REEM. I've had enough of you and this house! You think I'm doing this just to fuck with you?

NADIA. Why else? You must be enjoying this.

REEM. No, Nadia, I'm not enjoying this. I don't enjoy this at all! I told you I want to sell this house and will do everything I can to make that happen!

NADIA. Bravo! You'll have to show me how clever you are then!

REEM. So, we're still in the same place! You insist on this torture! Shall we have this out in the courts? Is that what you want?

NADIA. What do you think you'll get from taking me to court? If I don't agree, you'll never sell the house!

REEM. Once I get Nabeel on my side, we'll force you to sell!

NADIA. Don't worry, Nabeel would never do that…

REEM. Really? Are you sure about that?

NADIA. Not just Nabeel, his wife too!

REEM. Oh, really?

NADIA. Honestly! She loves her money, and I've found a way to keep her satisfied.

REEM. Liar!

NADIA. Go on, ask her.

REEM. Are you trying to scare me?

NADIA. Suit yourself. You'll find out soon enough.

REEM. What did you do? What did you say to Nabeel?

NADIA. Ask him.

REEM. I'm asking you.

NADIA. I've signed off my share of the inheritance to him, on the condition that I get to stay in this house for the rest of my life.

REEM. What do you mean?

NADIA. Nabeel owns two-thirds of this house now, and in return, he agreed to let me live in it until I die. That means, if you want to sell this house, you'll have to do it over my dead body.

REEM. You had no right to do that…

NADIA. Says who?

REEM. You can't do this!

NADIA. Fine, ask your lawyer about it, and then get back to me…

REEM. You must be very pleased with yourself. Do you feel strong and intelligent now? I will ask my lawyer, we'll contest this, and we'll see what you can do about that!

NADIA. Well, I'd like to see what you can do! Do you know how long a case like this could take? Ten years, at least. You'll lose, anyway…

REEM. We'll see about that! What do you know?

NADIA. Whatever you say, Reem. You can do whatever makes you happy, if you can…

REEM. Of course I can. Even if it means dragging this through the courts for ten, twenty, fifty years. I'll persist with this from my grave. Whatever it takes, this house will be sold.

*End of Act One.*

## ACT TWO

### Scene One

NADIA *and* NABEEL *are in the living room.*

NADIA. What does that mean?

NABEEL. It's over, you have to leave the house…

NADIA. I can't even comprehend it…

NABEEL. I know… But there's nothing more we can do…

NADIA. I don't understand… Suddenly they want to build a new highway? All of a sudden there's Town Planning involved.

NABEEL. Well, it's not much of surprise, Nadia. Didn't you hear the lawyer say this project had been lost for fifty years – (*Mocking.*) 'If not since the time of the Ottomans…' Our beloved Government has been busy with Solidere for so long, and just now they remember all their other town planning.

NADIA. I don't care about all the roads they're building. What does our house have to do with it?

NABEEL. It's right in the middle of the planned highway. If Your Highness had agreed to sell it a year ago, we would've made some real money! Now, we'll be lucky to get forty or fifty per cent of what it's worth!

NADIA. As little as forty or fifty?

NABEEL. Something about the highway only running through half the house! Just our luck!

NADIA. You can stop talking about it now. It's painful enough…

NABEEL. If you'd only accepted when Reem wanted to sell the house last year. But no! You wanted to stay! You're stubborn and unbreakable!

NADIA. Now it's my fault? I seem to remember you loved it when I gave you my share of the house.

NABEEL. I only wanted what's best for you! You were on the verge of breaking down. There was no talking to you... But you're always right, whatever you do, you're always right. Whatever happens you're always right...

NADIA. Don't blame me for your lacking in the testicles department! If you really wanted to sell this place, you could've stamped your foot and sold it with Reem regardless!

NABEEL. Not one more word! I could kill you!

NADIA. I'll speak to Reem... We'll see what we can do about this. Maybe we can take this to court, appeal or whatever...

NABEEL. Nadia, the decision comes from the Ministry. What can you do? Aren't you tired of this already? Or do you want to waste more time until the value drops further?!

NADIA. Stop blaming me! Did I plan to build this bloody highway? What am I supposed to do? What's done is done, let's try to find a solution, some legal loophole...

NABEEL. There is no solution, Nadia, and I don't want to be wasting any more money on lawyers, or getting into any 'legal loopholes' with you... In seven, eight months, a year at the most, they'll pay us our money, you'll leave the house, and they'll finally demolish this place. We take whatever they offer, because no one's going to buy it from us anyway...

NADIA. It's not about finding someone to buy it. It's about buying us more time...

NABEEL. 'More time'? You'll have to leave sooner or later. Enough! Forget about it! Let go of this cursed house!

NADIA. Can you please just listen to me? Reem knows many important people, she might be able to help us...

NABEEL. Reem, help you? She was dying to get rid of this house. Or has that conveniently slipped your mind?

NADIA. Reem wanted to sell. I don't think she'd be happy with the Ministry running a highway through the place and drip-feeding us money...

NABEEL. Either way, we lose.

NADIA. We have to call Reem. I'll speak to her.

NABEEL. When will you stop fighting this? Till the last breath *ya'ni*?

NADIA. I'm fighting for my home, Nabeel. I don't expect you to understand.

NABEEL. Of course. You're the only one who lives here, only you understand!

*He starts to leave.*

NADIA. You're just going to sit back while they take our house away?

NABEEL. There's nothing more we can do. I'm not dealing with this any more.

**Scene Two**

*Inside the house, empty of most of its furniture. Suitcases and boxes in the corners.* NADIA *brings some bags down from the upstairs rooms. The front door is open.* REEM *enters.* NADIA *sees her, runs towards her, and hugs her.*

NADIA. I'm glad you came. I missed you...

REEM (*quietly*). How are you, Nadia? Everything packed?

NADIA. Almost. The movers came and took the furniture to the new house. All your things are over there. (*She points to a corner.*)

REEM. Do you need any help?

NADIA. No, I'm done. That's it...

REEM. What about the furniture that's left?

NADIA. Not enough space for it in the new house. I'll put them in Nabeel's garage, he can sell them if he wants to...

REEM *looks around, observing the space.*

Can you believe it, Reem? I can feel my heart breaking inside... I can't believe I'm leaving this place...

REEM (*noticing another pile of things in a corner*). Are those mine as well?

NADIA. They're Nabeel's. Have you seen him?

REEM. Not yet.

NADIA. Have you spoken to him?

REEM. Yesterday, after I got back.

NADIA. What did he say?

REEM. What else would he say? That you're leaving the house in three days...

NADIA. Didn't he say we should've sold the house, just like you wanted?

REEM. He called me in Qatar to tell me about the highway. He was very upset.

NADIA. He blames me for it... but things happen, you know. I just couldn't bring myself to leave this house...

REEM. It's done now. No use talking about it...

*She moves some things closer to the door.*

NADIA. Will you come and visit me at my new place?

REEM. If I'm invited...

NADIA (*smiles*). I'm not sure if I'll get used to it, the new house... I don't know what to do...

REEM. You'll get used to it, Nadia! You've survived worse. What's wrong with you?

NADIA. I feel as though the world is ending... You know? I don't regret not selling the house... At least I had those two years of living here...

REEM. You really don't regret it? With all the money we've lost? We only got half of what it's worth!

*Silence.*

Just so you could stay here those two years, you put me, yourself and Nabeel through hell? All the lawyers and court-rooms... and you still don't regret it? Well, I don't regret it either, I don't regret it at all.

NADIA. Of course you don't! When did you ever regret stirring up trouble...? In any case, you got what you wanted. You wanted to get rid of this place and you couldn't sell it, now the Government's snatched it away... You always get what you want... It's a game of luck...

REEM. Yes, luck. You're right, it's all just a game of luck.

REEM *moves the rest of her things to the door.*

NADIA. What can we do? In our family we're destined for pain…

REEM. You know what, Nadia? If you think sometimes other people have it easy, you're not mistaken. You'd be right, other people out there do get what they want, their lives are much easier. But if you think this thing just fell out of the sky to torture you and make me happy, you'd be very wrong about that. I worked hard to make this happen!

NADIA. What?!

REEM. You heard me! If you think the Government woke up to a long-lost piece of town planning overnight, I'll have you know they had someone to remind them!

NADIA. I don't believe this! You took your twisted ways all the way up to the Ministry? You liar!

REEM. I'm not lying! My 'twisted ways'? You remember my Shi'ite boyfriend? Majid… Remember how he wanted to marry me but Mama and his parents wouldn't have it? He went to study abroad and I had a nervous breakdown? Well, Majid's now an engineer working for the Ministry, and we're still friends…

NADIA. So it's that easy? You tell your ex-boyfriend and he tears down the house?

REEM. Of course it wasn't that easy, Nadia… I spent God knows how long trying to convince him. He doesn't like this sort of thing, but I have my ways… I'd heard about this piece of planning a long time ago. Remember Mama saying there was a highway that was going to run right through this house? Baba thought it would take them a hundred years to get the Government contracts signed? We dug up the highway plan, and found a minister to sign off on it, we looked for support in very high places… If Majid had enough power to get this done himself, it wouldn't have taken a year or two…

NADIA. I can't even begin to believe what I'm hearing…

REEM. I'm sorry, Nadia. You forced me to do it like this…

NADIA. No, of course I didn't.

REEM. Can you imagine the highway cutting through this living room? We might be left with just a corner of the kitchen, or half a wall… but I think they'll demolish the whole thing. (*Very excited.*) The cars will rip right through here – (*She points in the direction of the future traffic.*) at a hundred and twenty kilometres per hour… The living room, everything above it. The spare room, your room, Mama's room… It'll be open unto the sky… Lovely. Like being in a convertible. Aaaaah… Breathe, Nadia, breathe it in… The fresh air. Finally… It's all happening.

NADIA. How could you do this, Reem? How could you?

REEM. It's the happiest ending! You know if we'd sold it, and they'd turned it into a hotel or a restaurant, the walls would still be standing. But now it'll be gone. Eradicated. There will be nothing left. Can you imagine it? Can you see it, Nadia? It's all over!

NADIA. Yes, I can imagine… I see…

REEM. Congratulations, Nadia, congratulations.

*The End.*

# EGYPTIAN PRODUCTS
منتجات مصرية

LAILA SOLIMAN

*translated by*

KHALID LAITH

*To my father…*
*whose loneliness I now understand*

*L.S.*

## Laila Soliman

Laila Soliman is an independent Egyptian theatre director and playwright, living and working in Cairo. She graduated from the American University in Cairo in 2004 with a degree in Theatre and Arabic Literature. Shortly after, she directed Naomi Wallace's *Retreating World*. In 2006, she staged *Ghorba, images of alienation*, an original text based on a process of improvisation with the actors of the play. In 2008, she worked as a dramaturg on Swiss director's Stefan Kaegi's documentary theatre piece *Radio Muezzin*. In 2009, she directed *...At your service!*, a play based on an adaptation of two plays by Harold Pinter and Fo/Rame at the Hanager Theatre, Cairo. In 2010, she wrote and directed the first Arabic adaptation of Frank Wedekind's *Spring Awakening*, staged in Egypt.

## Khalid Laith

Originally from the island of Bahrain in the Persian Gulf, Khalid Laith grew up and was educated between the Middle East, the UK and the United States. He trained as an actor at the Central School of Speech and Drama in London, where he currently lives. Next to his acting work, Khalid works as a translator in various fields, he edits short films and documentaries, and composes and produces his own music.

*Egyptian Products* was first performed as a rehearsed reading as part of the *I Come From There: New Plays from the Arab World* season in the Jerwood Theatre Upstairs, Royal Court Theatre, London, on 12 November 2008, with the following cast:

| | |
|---|---|
| HADIA | Michelle Terry |
| GASIR | Rudi Dharmalingham |
| USTAZ IDRIS | Raad Rawi |
| OTHERS | Jonathan McGuinness |
| *Director* | Hettie Macdonald |

The play was also read at Masrah Al Madina in Beirut, Lebanon, in January 2009.

158

## Characters

HADIA, *a young woman in her late twenties who suffers from a lack of an emotional life. She works as a nurse/companion to the Ustaz. The word* hadia *in Arabic means 'she who is calm'*

GASIR, *a young man in his early thirties, an introvert, who works in a medical lab and suffers from loneliness after the death of his mother. 'Gasir' is the Egyptian pronunciation of the Arabic name 'Jasir'. The word* jasir *in Arabic means 'he who is heroically brave'*

USTAZ IDRIS, *an elderly writer who is relatively famous, and well off. He suffers from loneliness and a few medical illnesses related to his old age. Ustaz is a term used for a learned elder*

*Also a* SPICE SELLER, *a female* LINGERIE-SHOP ASSISTANT, *four* PSYCHOTHERAPISTS, *a* TAXI DRIVER, *who can all be cast singly or doubled by one male and one female actor*

## Setting

The set comprises two sections: the writer's house, and another changeable space that transforms into various locations (a kitchen, a hotel toilet, a spice shop, a women's lingerie shop, a taxi, the offices of four different psychological therapists, a coffee shop, a restaurant, and a supermarket). The playwright suggests placing only the important pieces of furniture for each place on the stage in a random fashion and moving them in whichever way the director chooses to shape the scene.

## Notes and references

*Al Agooza* – an area in Cairo. Translates literally into 'the old lady' or 'the old woman'

*Elhamdulillah* – 'thank God' or 'thanks be to God'

*Hagg* – elderly man

*Haram* – religiously forbidden

*Inshallah* – God willing

*Mansoura* – Al Mansoura. A city in Egypt with a population of 420,000

*Suad Husni* – an Egyptian film star from the sixties and seventies

*Temporary marriage* or *zawaj urfi* – in some forms of Islam it is acceptable for couples to have a temporary marriage. It is a marriage contract with an expiration date used by young couples as a way for them to have sex without breaking religious law

*Trousseau* – the clothes, household linen, and other belongings collected by a bride for her marriage

*Wallahi* – I swear, 'I swear to you'

*W'allaikum essallam* – 'May the peace and blessing of Allah be upon you too', used in reply to '*Essallam allakaikum*'

*Ya'ni* – has several uses. Gasir's on page 167 is 'I mean'; Ustaz's on page 175 is 'meaning'; Gasir's second use on page 226 is 'sort of' (can also mean 'you mean')


There is a play on words on page 175 when Hadia and Ustaz are discussing Mahmoud Al Ghunaimi which doesn't quite translate. *Ghanam* translates as 'lamb' in Arabic, and Ghunaimi is a family name. The joke, then, is akin to:

USTAZ. What about that Joe the Lamb?

HADIA. You mean, Joe Lambert.

The poem Gasir and Ustaz recite on page 161, beginning 'With you living, my life would be fulfilling', is an extract from an Arabic Jahiliyyah poem by Maymun Ibn Qays Al-a'sha.

The song referred to that Gasir sings on page 161 is an Arabic children's song, written by Salah Jaheen and performed by Suad Husni.

The poem Gasir recites on pages 201 and 202 is a translated extract adapted from *Qais and Layla* (*Majnun Laila*) by Ahmed Shawqi, translated by Jeanette W.S. Atiya, GEBO, 1990; and *Leila and the Madman* (*Laila wal-Majnoun*) by Salah Abdul-Sabour, translated by M. Enani, GEBO, 1999.

Layla literally means 'mad for Layla' or 'driven mad by Layla'. According to legend, Qais went mad writing about his long-lost forbidden lover separated from him because of tribal feudalism, and came to be known as Majnoun Layla. It is the classic Arabic *Romeo and Juliet* story.

The poem Gasir recites on page 219, beginning 'Although she is now distant', is an extract from a poem by Abul Hassan al-Karkhi.

The poem Gasir recites on page 219, beginning 'You are far, yet close in my sweet torment', is an extract from a poem by Sufi poet Mansur al-Hallaj.

**Prologue**

*Two separate spots of light on a dark stage.* GASIR *in one,* HADIA *in the other.*

GASIR *carries a suitcase along with various other bits and bobs which belonged to his late mother. He seems hesitant, inspecting each item and wondering whether he should pack it away.*

HADIA *is on her phone.*

GASIR *and* USTAZ.
 With you living, my life would be fulfilling.
 And if you cease, then no life after you would be worth
  living.

HADIA (*agitated*). Okay, Mama!

USTAZ (*off*). Hadia. Who wrote this poem?

GASIR (*to the tune of the Arabic song*). Oh, Mother. Oh, Mummy. Oh, Mama.

USTAZ. Is he Egyptian?

HADIA. No, Mama!

GASIR. Salutations. Adorations. I kiss you!

USTAZ (*louder*). Hadia! Where are you, Hadia?

HADIA. Yes, coming. *Wallahi* I'm coming. (*Impatiently.*) Okay, all right, Mama.

USTAZ. What are you doing, Hadia?

GASIR. This day is yours, my only lady.

USTAZ (*forceful yet fearful*). Hadia?

HADIA (*on the verge of a breakdown*). Coming!

> *She speaks as* GASIR *slams the suitcase shut.*

> *Blackout.*

### Scene One

HADIA *walks in a directionless and violent manner.* GASIR *enters from the opposite direction. We realise they are both headed towards the herb and spice shop (selling traditional spices, perfumes and herbal remedies). The shop's shelves are stocked with colourful bottles of herbs and oils, measuring scales, etc. Hundreds of little signs indicate the healing properties of each potion.*

SELLER (*to* GASIR). Good to see you, sir. Haven't seen you in a while. We haven't upset you, have we?

> HADIA *heads towards the* SELLER, *cutting in front of* GASIR, *convinced it is her right, because ladies are always first.* GASIR *shyly waits his turn.*

HADIA (*attracting the* SELLER's *attention*). Good evening.

> GASIR *is silent.*

SELLER (*annoyed*). W'allaikum essallam, Allah's blessings be upon you too.

HADIA. I need an ointment for rheumatism, please.

> *The* SELLER *gets the ointment.*

And a laxative mixture.

> *The* SELLER *fetches the mixture.*

No, no, the one made with prunes. (*Agitated.*) Are you new here or what?!

SELLER. No, no, God forgive me.

*The* SELLER *looks for the right mixture.*

HADIA'*s phone rings.*

HADIA (*on the phone*). Hello. Yes, Ustaz. How are you? Feeling the same… Yes, I'm at the spice seller's.

*The* SELLER *takes advantage of the phone call to talk to* GASIR. *He smiles at him questioningly.*

SELLER. How can I help you? Something for yourself this time?

GASIR (*sadly*). Yes, I am looking for something… (*He becomes flustered.*)

SELLER. What? (*Whispers.*) Go on…

GASIR *starts to speak.*

Some hippo lotion? (*He winks at* GASIR.)

GASIR (*defending himself against the accusation*). No, no.

HADIA (*on the phone*). Yes, I've got the ointment and the laxative. Do you need anything else?

GASIR. No, I just need –

SELLER (*encouraging him*). Yes?

HADIA (*on the phone*). Okay. This prostate remedy, what's it called?

GASIR. I need something to help with my apprehensions, if you catch my drift.

HADIA (*on the phone*). Okay, I'll look for it.

SELLER. I understand you… Natural Viagra…

GASIR. No!

*HADIA hears the word 'Viagra'. She ends the call and is frustrated to find that the* SELLER *is helping* GASIR *instead of her.*

HADIA. Excuse me! I'm not done yet. I also need a herbal prostate remedy.

SELLER. What kind?

HADIA. It's green, apparently.

SELLER. Which one?

HADIA. You should know, shouldn't you?!

SELLER (*cold and sarcastically*). Sorry, I don't…

HADIA. Where's the *hagg* who owns this place?

SELLER. He went out to pray…

> HADIA*'s phone rings again, just as she's about to start an argument. She tries to regain her composure before answering.*

HADIA (*on the phone*). Yes, Ustaz.

> *The* SELLER *takes advantage of the phone call to turn his attention to* GASIR *once more.*

SELLER. So… Tell me. What was it you were looking for?

HADIA (*on the phone*). You can't be serious?! I can't ask him about that!

GASIR. I'm looking for…

HADIA (*on the phone*). Okay. I'll ask him if it has any effect on… (*Whispering.*) your unmentionables.

SELLER. What? Something to stiffen your resolve? (*Another wink.*)

GASIR. No, no, please! I've got enough on my plate.

HADIA (*on the phone*). A sedative, and a general energiser. Anything else? Something to regulate your blood pressure. What else?

GASIR. It's just that I get so nervous, you know.

HADIA (*on the phone*). An artery dilator…

SELLER. Yes, I know. *Wallahi* I understand you. You mean, you're embarrassed.

GASIR. No, you're misunderstanding me.

HADIA (*on the phone*). Sure and –

*It appears the caller has rudely hung up.*

SELLER. There's nothing to be scared of. These herbs have no harmful side effects.

*HADIA turns to the SELLER. The phone call has drained her of all patience.*

HADIA. Do you mind staying with me so we can finish here?

GASIR (*in another world*). I'm sorry but –

HADIA. It's just never-ending today!

*The scene freezes for a moment. GASIR then springs towards HADIA to kiss her. She fully responds to the kiss, as if it were a scene from an eighties' kitsch romantic film. Intense passion. The SELLER smiles ecstatically. The 'happily ever after' ending. Suddenly, they revert to their original postures and positions. HADIA becomes more intense, as though GASIR has just sexually harassed her. GASIR becomes nervous.*

(*To* GASIR.) Please. I was first, and it's very obvious you don't even know what you want – (*Insinuating that what he's asking for is illegal.*) and in all honesty, I've had enough of the heat in this place. I'm getting claustrophobic.

GASIR (*embarrassed whisper*). I'm sorry.

HADIA (*hasn't heard him and carries on like a loose cannon*). Give me the green prostate medicine and some sedatives and a general enhancer – general, you hear, not sexual – and a blood-pressure stabiliser – Oh, and some calming antidepressants.

SELLER. For yourself?

HADIA. Why?! Do I look like I need it?! (*She turns to* GASIR *again, remembering his presence*.) And why are you standing so close? You've been standing here for an hour not knowing what you want. You're choking me. The last thing I need is you rubbing up against me. Oh, just go drink some mint tea or something!

SELLER. Miss, the tranquilliser!

**Scene Two**

GASIR *is at home, on the phone.*

GASIR (*in a shy voice*). Hello, good morning – I mean, good evening. Is this the problem number that's been advertised? I mean, is this the problem hotline? I mean, the one we call to discuss our problems... My name? I'm... I'm... G.D.

So, do I just talk or do you ask questions?

No. *Elhamdulillah* I work. Uh, I work in a medical lab. My problem... My problem is that I don't know what to do with my mother's things. I can't even bring myself to wash her pillow. No, she passed away three months ago – long may you live too – and I was very attached to her. I haven't slept properly in weeks, and everything's confusing me. I've been having some very strange dreams. I wake up in the mornings, not knowing where I am or what day it is, sometimes I don't sleep at all, other times I just sleep through the whole day. Oh, and it takes me a while to gather myself after, especially if I've seen her in my dreams. So, I wake up and smell her perfume and pillow, and I even carry pieces of it around in my pocket to sniff throughout the day... Do you know much about dreams?

No, I'm not married. No, of course my mother didn't mind. I suppose it wasn't meant to be... or the circumstances didn't allow. So, you don't know much about dreams? No. That's only the half of it, you see, sometimes I have this other sort of dream. I'm a little embarrassed... I have this problem with my energy levels... Uh... You're a man and you understand me, of course. I sit for hours after I wake up... Umm... Well, sometimes I'm forced to be late for work, or wake up earlier than usual just so I can... Hello, hello? Yes. You understand me, of course. I can't even talk to a girl without dreaming about her later and – Umm... I get very shy, you see... and worried that – Uh... *Ya'ni* – Hello? Hello, can you hear me? – No, I'm thirty-two. When did I hit puberty? Don't remember... a long time ago. You understand me, don't you? – No, but where do you think the problem is? My trousers? But I've tried everything in that area. I've tried them tight, I've tried them loose. Do you think the fabric might be the problem? Hello, can you hear me? Hello – Hello!

*We hear hysterical laughter on the other end of the phone as he pulls it away from his ear.*

### Scene Three

*The* USTAZ *is at home lying in his big comfy chair. He never leaves the stage.* HADIA *fidgets with her phone until she gets a text message which the audience hears, or sees on a screen.*

MALE VOICE. 'Life isn't easy. Please understand that I have to protect myself from you. And you too must protect yourself from me.'

HADIA *tosses the phone aside.*

USTAZ. I'm craving some potato chips.

HADIA. You know you're not allowed.

USTAZ. But I'm absolutely craving them...

HADIA. Sorry, not allowed.

USTAZ. I'm the one who decides what I'm allowed or not and my stomach's been good today...

HADIA. But the doctor said you're not allowed.

USTAZ. What does he know?! My blood sugar's low and my body needs some potato chips.

HADIA (*sarcastically*). Oh, really? Never heard that one before...

USTAZ. I've already got one foot in the grave... And, anyway, I don't understand why you're so agitated.

HADIA. I'm not agitated.

USTAZ. I know you're agitated because that new boy's dumped you. Right?

HADIA. Of course not. And I'm not agitated.

USTAZ. No. Agitated. But it was clear from the start that he wasn't good enough for you. Too simple-minded. You're far more intelligent than he is. In my opinion...

HADIA. Excuse me, but what exactly brought this up? You're making something out of nothing.

USTAZ. You're far too eager to get married and it would be best for you to –

HADIA. I never mentioned marriage –

USTAZ. It would be best for you to postpone these sort of thoughts.

HADIA. And why is that?

USTAZ. So you can enjoy your life –

HADIA (*sarcastically*). Like I'm enjoying it right now.

USTAZ. Before some stupid man takes control of you.

HADIA *gives him a surprised look.*

Because marriage is –

HADIA (*finishing his sentence*). – a failed institution.

USTAZ. My advice is that you should take up yoga…

HADIA (*losing patience*). Hmmm.

USTAZ. The best thing for you now is yoga!

> HADIA *is irritated and starts flipping through a magazine.*

Nothing will help you… except for yoga!

> *Every repetition of the word irritates* HADIA *further. She bottles it in.*

Okay, fetch me – (*He indicates the number with his fingers.*) three breadsticks.

HADIA. No, you're not supposed to have any.

USTAZ. But I really want some.

HADIA. For God's sake…

USTAZ. All right then, two. (*He indicates with his fingers.*)

HADIA. No.

USTAZ. How about one?

HADIA. No!

USTAZ (*with childish petulance*). I hate you.

HADIA. Suit yourself.

USTAZ. What's so wrong with eating what I want? I've been taking my insulin, and even if –

HADIA. I've had enough. Do we have to battle and barter for everything?

USTAZ. Even if my blood sugar stays low, I'll still have to take the insulin.

HADIA. This is impossible. This is seriously impossible.

USTAZ. I know why you're so agitated like this. Serves me right for hiring women.

HADIA. Right!

*She starts to gather her things, but changes her mind and sits back down.*

USTAZ. That's it. Leave. I don't want you any more. You've given me a headache!

*She turns her back to the* USTAZ.

Hadia, what are you doing?

*No answer.*

Hadia!

*No answer.*

Are you upset now?

*No answer.*

Hadia! Hadia! Hadia!

HADIA. Yes?

USTAZ. What are you doing?

*Silence.*

Hadia!

HADIA *sits there in total silence.*

What the hell are you doing, Hadia?

HADIA. Yoga… I'm doing some yoga…

## Scene Four

GASIR *is in a taxi, sitting in the passenger seat.*

TAXI DRIVER. So, where you heading today?

GASIR. Al Agooza.

TAXI DRIVER. Old women, young girls; a hole's a hole, eh?! (*He laughs out loud.*) Why aren't you laughing? Don't make it so complicated, tomorrow's another day.

GASIR. Hmm.

TAXI DRIVER. Looks like the wife's left you in a bad mood this morning, if you don't mind me saying.

GASIR *doesn't answer.*

Speaking of the wife at home, how about a joke? (*He doesn't give* GASIR *a chance to answer.*) Here's one. Before marriage you do the talking and she listens, after marriage she does all the talking and you listen, and after three years you both do the talking and the whole wide world listens. (*He chuckles.*) Ah, relax, mate, it can't be that bad. All right, listen to this, it's a good one... A taxi driver, like myself, gets bored of his wife, takes an ad out in the paper saying: 'Looking to exchange. One wife in good condition... Plush interiors... Recently overhauled bosom... Firm hips... With a mileage of only ten thousand nights...' (*He laughs alone.*) Eh? Don't you think that's funny? All women are a pain in the arse.

GASIR (*uptight*). I'm not married.

TAXI DRIVER (*sarcastically*). Oh, well, you haven't lived yet, that must be why you frown in the mornings. (*A sly smile crosses his face.*) 'Marriage completes religion,' or so they say. Believe me, I know how tough life is these days, how ruthless women can be with their demands. Stay single. Enjoy your life while you can.

I got another one for you. Viagra dosages.

– With a girl you've just met… No need.

– With your sweetheart… Half a pill.

– With your mistress… One pill.

– With your wife… Six pills, ten beers, three whiskies, two hash spliffs, and a skunk rocket and good luck to you… It's hit… or miss! (*He lets out a loud grotesque laugh.*) Hey, why aren't you laughing? Don't tell me you've never tried it…

GASIR. Tried what?

TAXI DRIVER. You man of experience, you.

GASIR (*losing his patience*). Experienced what?

TAXI DRIVER. Don't wind yourself up now… I've got just the pretty girl for you. Very clean. Satisfaction guaranteed.

GASIR *blushes with embarrassment.*

Or are girls not your thing? You gay? A bicycle, eh? (*Laughs.*) You like to be ridden?

GASIR. Could you let me out here, please…

TAXI DRIVER. Okay, but before you get down –

GASIR. Just here, please.

TAXI DRIVER (*laughs*). Fine, fine. But I could always arrange that ride, you know. (*Continues to laugh.*)

GASIR (*distressed*). Just let me off here!

## Scene Five

HADIA *is in the* USTAZ*'s bedroom, on the phone.*

HADIA. Hello... *Allaikum essallam*, Mama. How are you? How's everyone doing? Well, I'm not really sure when I can take the time off work.

USTAZ (*in a loud voice*). You can take a vacation whenever you want.

*She gestures for him to be quiet.*

HADIA (*on the phone*). And who's this new groom then? Who chose him this time? Mama, you know this type of marriage doesn't suit me. I don't really want to get married in Mansoura. Why? What's wrong with me working here?! For God's sake, the man I work for is older than my father, Mama.

USTAZ. Thank you!

HADIA (*she covers the phone*). I'm sorry.

*She gestures to him: 'You understand.'*

(*On the phone.*) Okay, fine, we'll see what happens... Mama, my brothers can say whatever they like, they're not turning me into a walking black tent like they did their wives... I'll have you know I dress very modestly. I'm not walking around naked, flashing my bits... You too, Mama?!

USTAZ. So, what's she saying? What's she saying?

HADIA (*on the phone*). No, I haven't forgotten how old I am... I'm twenty-nine, there's no need to humiliate me like this.

USTAZ (*impassioned*). She has no right.

HADIA (*on the phone*). Now you're threatening me?! You're threatening me, Mama. Mama, please, I'm not a child any more.

USTAZ. What? What's she threatening you with?

HADIA (*on the phone*). Don't worry, Mama. Of course, Mama… Sure… Of course… *W'allaikum essallam*, Mama.

USTAZ. So, what did she say to you?

HADIA. You know… The usual… Except now there's a count-down.

USTAZ. I don't understand. Are they angry because you're working for me?

HADIA. That's not the issue… Mama's worried the marriage train's going to pass me by, and my brothers are worried about their reputation.

USTAZ. What about their reputation?

HADIA. Their sister is in Cairo working for a single man, whom she happens to live with. That's not an easy one to swallow in a town like Mansoura, or anywhere else for that matter. What will people say?

USTAZ. How do these people think?! You know, they must have heard about my reputation with the ladies and are just afraid for you.

HADIA (*with a smile*). I don't think so…

USTAZ. Or maybe your brother read one of the anti-religious books I've written?

HADIA. I really don't think so…

USTAZ. So, what did your mother threaten you with?

HADIA. If I don't get engaged by the time I'm thirty, I have to go back to Mansoura so they can find me a husband.

USTAZ. What? And what am I supposed to do?

HADIA *gives him a sharp look.*

I mean, how dare she?! This is a serious problem. We must find a solution.

HADIA. Hmm…

USTAZ. Let's put our heads together…

HADIA *doesn't answer.*

You want us to pretend to get married? You and me?

HADIA. Of course not.

USTAZ. You'll get my pension when I die…

HADIA. Even so. No.

USTAZ. Well… What do you think of that lawyer, Abdel Galil?

HADIA. Definitely not.

USTAZ. Why not? He's a good man and…

HADIA. Too sleazy.

USTAZ. Fine, forget him. What about that Mahmoud Al Ghanam?

HADIA. You mean, Al Ghunaimi.

USTAZ. Yes, the one who's doing his Masters on my writings, he's an intelligent man, with impeccable taste and –

HADIA. And no, thank you. I wouldn't want to marry him. Besides, I don't think he's interested.

USTAZ. Okay then. What about –

HADIA. Are you playing matchmaker now?

USTAZ. Why not? Just arrange a sham marriage to get your mother off your back, so you can stay with me… and then, after some time, break off the engagement –

HADIA (*laughs*). No way.

USTAZ (*sadly*). Do you really want to get married then?

HADIA. Yes.

USTAZ. *Ya'ni* you'll leave me?

HADIA. I'll come and visit.

USTAZ. Well, at least marry someone I know.

HADIA. The youngest person who comes round here, whom you call 'a child', is at least fifty years old.

USTAZ. And what's wrong with marrying a man in his fifties?

HADIA. Not for me. But I will try to marry someone who likes you…

*He begins to calm down.*

USTAZ. I can see that nothing will brighten your mood except for some of that Swiss chocolate I was sent. And how about rewarding ourselves with a glass of whiskey too?

HADIA. You know I don't drink… (*Referring to his health.*) It's also not allowed.

USTAZ. Have you even tried it?

HADIA. I don't have to try everything.

USTAZ. How can you be so quick to judge something you haven't even –

HADIA. Because Allah says 'Know the Halal from the *Haram*.' And this is *Haram*!

USTAZ. But Allah –

HADIA. No, no, no. *Haram* means *Haram*. We can't pick and choose with religion.

USTAZ. You haven't even tried it…

## Scene Six

HADIA *is in the bathroom, making herself up before going out.*

GASIR *is in the men's toilet, in some hotel.*

GASIR. My God, what is this? I knew I shouldn't have come to this wedding. I'm not one for weddings, anyway. How can anyone go to a wedding when they just buried their mother three months ago? *Wallahi* it's just to please you, Mama. It's absolute chaos out there. What a headache! Of course I won't meet anyone here. This is no atmosphere for falling in love.

HADIA *rings her mother as she removes the veil from her head.*

HADIA. Hello, yes, Mama. Tell you what, I don't think I'll be able to make it today. The Ustaz has been very poorly and I can't bring myself to leave him alone. Oh, you know, one of those aches he gets. No, it's not sudden, it happens all the time, Mama. He's eighty years old and having a severe pain attack. What am I supposed to do?! Leave him alone?! No, I'm not lying to you! Okay, Mama, of course. Goodbye.

GASIR. Maybe if I'd been drafted into the army my problems would've been solved by now, as they say. I'd be surrounded by friends. People would see me as a real man and stop calling me 'nice' and 'well-mannered'. Maybe if I'd flirted with the neighbour's daughter – on the phone – or through the window – or even from the balcony. No, how could I?! But if I'd played out in the street, like the other boys, and learned to fight – I could've been – talking dirty to the girls and whistling at them as they passed... I would've stayed out late and disappeared for days – but Mama would've worried.

HADIA*'s phone rings.*

HADIA. Yes, Mama. *W'allaikum essallam.* Mama, I've just finished work. Mama, I swear if you rush me one more time – Fine, I didn't mean to. Mama, I'm sorry. Okay... *W'allaikum essallam*, Mama.

*She puts her veil back on.*

God, why does it have to be like this? Why can't you send me a decent man to save me from all this? Do all of them have to be losers?! A man can be forty and still be a child, with no idea what he wants... and if he already knows what he wants, then he's usually up to no good. Disgusting.

GASIR. How does it concern me who bought their dress where and how much it cost them? 'That girl got her gown specially made for the wedding,' as if it's the dress that'll catch her a husband. And my aunt tells me Hazem's bride insisted he invite all his bachelor friends to the wedding. 'Come, my dear, Aunt So-and-so, you remember her, mother of So-and-so, wants to meet you,' only to be cornered at every angle with questions and answers – your job, your age, your flat, your family... No, no...! Damn it... It's upsetting my stomach...

*He feels nauseous but cannot vomit.*

HADIA. It could work out – I have to be optimistic. It's still possible that I'll find someone suitable, unlike the deranged men I keep meeting. They say I'm spoiled!! What do you call all those primmed and preened girls then? And even if it doesn't work out, maybe Mama will finally realise God is fair, and marriage just isn't as easy as frying eggs. Then we'll see how much better they can do.

GASIR *heads for the door to exit but is stopped by the loud sound of the wedding procession outside.*

GASIR. I think I'll wait until they pass... I don't want my aunt making any more of her ridiculous suggestions. 'Gasir, my dear, Omar Makram Mosque offers a great service. You give them your details and a description of what qualities you're looking for in a life-partner, and they bring together like-minded people under God's law.' No, no... My God.

HADIA. No... I can't stand another sitting-room meet-and-greet. I'm not going.

*She starts to take off her veil and change her clothes.*

GASIR. No, no, I'm not leaving here until that commotion's over.

*He sits on the closed toilet seat.* HADIA*'s phone rings again.*

HADIA. Hello. Yes, Mama. No, I'm not coming today. Don't start swearing at me. I can't believe you're all setting this trap for me! Again! Wasn't it enough my brother's friend wanted me to change the way I dress, how I look and everything else about myself? And after all of that, he says, 'Sorry, I need a more religious mother for my children.' Look, Mother. I'm not coming. Tell my brothers – and yourself – to relax because I'm not getting married in this way. Don't you even dare think of finding me a husband again!!

GASIR. What is this? How do people sit on this filthy thing?

*He starts to clean the toilet seat.*

**Scene Seven**

*This scene is a pastiche of several separate little scenes between* HADIA *and the* USTAZ, *and* GASIR *and the* THERA-PISTS. *These scenes are closer to a nightmare than reality. The scene contains text messages from various men to* HADIA, *which the director can either project onto a screen or have recorded using different voices.* HADIA *sits with the* USTAZ *at his house, she fiddles with her phone, deleting text messages from previous suitors.* GASIR *visits various* THERAPISTS.

MALE VOICE. 'You are not the one to carry the burden of my pain. You are the essence of a spoiled brat. I'm looking for a real woman, and you're nothing more than a cheap advertisement of one.'

HADIA (*to herself*). Delete.

USTAZ. Will you cry if die?

HADIA. What sort of question is that? Of course I'll cry.

USTAZ. Do you think my daughter will cry for me?

HADIA. What are you like? Of course she will.

USTAZ. But my daughter doesn't call any more.

HADIA. She called you just this morning.

USTAZ. This morning? Oh, yes, I forgot. Do you think my new book will be well received?

HADIA. I imagine the book will be a huge success. (*Pause.*) Do you think I'll get married?

USTAZ. When? Before the book?

HADIA. No. Whenever...

USTAZ. Will you scratch my back?

*She leaves her phone and scratches his back with a back-scratcher.*

HADIA. There?

USTAZ. No, a little higher...

HADIA. So? Do you think I'll ever get married?

USTAZ. Yes, why not?! (*About the scratching.*) That's the spot.

*GASIR is with THERAPIST 1, who is busy at his desk, and increasingly losing patience with GASIR.*

THERAPIST 1. So, what problems do you have with the opposite sex?

GASIR. I don't know...

THERAPIST 1. Sorry, I can hardly hear you. What did you say?

GASIR. I don't know.

THERAPIST 1. When did you say your mother passed away?

GASIR. Three months ago...

THERAPIST 1. Hmm… Again, what are your problems with opposite sex?

GASIR. I'm not sure…

THERAPIST 1 (*losing his patience*). Look, do you have a problem or don't you?

GASIR *looks at* THERAPIST 1 *in fear.*

USTAZ. Aren't you going to eat with me?

HADIA. No, thank you.

USTAZ. Fine, I won't have anything either!

HADIA. No, really, I'm not hungry.

USTAZ. Maybe you're in love?

HADIA. No, it's just hot.

MAN'S VOICE. 'When you stop complicating things, call me. I know you want it… And I want you to be my – '

HADIA. That's enough of that. You too, in the trash…

HADIA *puts her frustrations into closing the phone, the* USTAZ *watches her.*

USTAZ. What was that man's name?

HADIA. What man?

USTAZ. I've told you a million times not to let a man take you out…

HADIA. Why?

USTAZ. So he doesn't ask you for more after dinner…

GASIR *with* THERAPIST 2, *a female.*

THERAPIST 2. You seem to be a decent young man with a suitable degree of self-esteem.

GASIR *shakes his head, unconvinced.*

So, let's get to the core of things, shall we? Tell me about your sex life.

GASIR *is shocked.*

Look, I think your shy and rattled behaviour, especially with the opposite sex, stems from an elemental inadequacy of the sexual kind. Consider me an older sister, you needn't be shy with me. 'No shame in science,' as they say. When do you think your problem with sex started?

GASIR *is silent.*

By the way, you remind me of my husband when we first met... (*Laughs.*) You too might only need a delicate woman like myself to bring you out of your shell.

MAN'S VOICE. 'It isn't true that deep inside I don't want you.'

HADIA. You can keep the deep. Delete. Goodbye.

USTAZ. You need someone well-established, who's confident in themselves.

HADIA (*lost in the phone*). Excuse me?

USTAZ. The good ones are very few and far between.

HADIA (*smiles*). So, what do I do?

MALE VOICE. 'Will you trust me enough to show you that place where I found my peace? Will you reject everything you've known, even yourself, to find something far more magnificent? That is what you have to do!'

HADIA. Ugh...

USTAZ. It's a cruel world...

HADIA. I agree.

USTAZ. No gentlemen left in it.

HADIA. Maybe you're right. But men aren't everything. I just want a baby...

USTAZ. That's another predicament. Even if you found a good man – and that's almost impossible, of course – how can you guarantee his DNA?

HADIA. What do you mean?

USTAZ. The most important qualities are intelligence and generosity. What if your son turned out to be stupid or stingy?

MALE VOICE (*continued from the previous message*). 'Sorry, I can't continue this. I need a more religious mother for my children.'

HADIA. Thank you very much…

GASIR *with* THERAPIST 3.

THERAPIST 3. You see, my son, your extreme attachment to your mother's belongings – her perfume, her clothes and pillow – indicates a possible issue with your sexual orientation…

GASIR. Sorry?!

THERAPIST 3. Why can't you accept the possibility of your homosexuality?

GASIR. Sorry?!

THERAPIST 3. You don't strike me as someone who's very sure about his attraction to women.

GASIR. But unfortunately I'm… I mean, I am sure.

GASIR *leaves*.

THERAPIST 3. Okay, go and get married if you think that'll help.

THERAPIST 3 *shakes his head and clucks in disapproval as* GASIR *runs off*.

USTAZ. You know, I've always been popular with the ladies. Many women used to chase after me.

## Scene Eight

*In the* USTAZ's *apartment. A long and silent exchange of glances between* HADIA *and* GASIR. HADIA *interrogates him with her looks.* GASIR *is embarrassed. The* USTAZ *is in the toilet.*

GASIR. Is the Ustaz in?

HADIA. Have we met before?! Yes. From the spice shop? What are you doing here? How dare you?!

GASIR (*interrupting*). I'm here about the medical tests.

HADIA (*embarrassed suddenly*). Oh. Excuse me. Please, come in.

GASIR. Is he here?

HADIA. Yes, of course. Have a seat.

USTAZ (*off*). Who is it, Hadia?

*She doesn't answer.*

Hadia! Who is it?

HADIA. He says he's here about the medical tests.

USTAZ (*off*). Well, let him in.

*No movement. The* USTAZ *comes in and sits in his chair.*

Come on... Let's get this over with.

GASIR. When did you have your last meal?

USTAZ. You're new. Where's Dr Magdi?

GASIR. Dr Magdi is on vacation. I'm replacing him while he's away.

USTAZ. But I've never seen you before. Isn't that right, Hadia? You're new!

GASIR. No. I've been working with Dr Magdi for the past eight years. When did you last eat, Ustaz?

USTAZ. He never told me about you. What's your name?

GASIR. Gasir, sir. When was your last meal?

HADIA. He's been fasting since the morning. For the tests.

*GASIR produces a syringe for taking a blood sample.*

Would you like something to drink?

*GASIR doesn't answer.*

What would you like to drink?

USTAZ (*seeing the syringe*). No, no, I don't have any more veins left for this. This isn't going to work... This isn't going to work... I don't want it. You're new. You look new.

*GASIR becomes nervous.*

HADIA. It's all right... Calm down. He's been doing this for eight years. Give him a chance.

USTAZ. Eight years?! I don't believe it! He can't have been doing this for eight years. How old are you?

GASIR. Thirty-two.

*Silence, before GASIR changes tactics.*

Don't worry. We can take a urine sample now, and postpone the blood test till later.

*HADIA is pleasantly surprised by his handling of the situation.*

USTAZ. Now, that's sensible. That makes sense.

*GASIR produces a plastic container from his briefcase.*

GASIR (*lowering his voice*). Please fill this up, Ustaz.

USTAZ. What?

GASIR (*louder*). Could you please fill this up.

USTAZ. I'll try, but I'm not sure I can...

*He exits.*

HADIA. He's just been, you see.

*Silence.*

He has to drink a lot of water because of his kidneys. My kidneys are quite weak even though I'm not old.

*Silence.*

They say these things are hereditary.

*Silence.*

How are your kidneys?

USTAZ (*off*). Hadia, ask him how much piss he needs…

GASIR *waits for* HADIA *to speak and ask the same question.* HADIA *ignores what the* USTAZ *has said.*

HADIA. I can understand it's a sensitive issue, seeing as it's hereditary – Makes you wonder what our children will take after us. You see, I think about that all the time – even though I don't have children – I'm not even married yet – But *elhamdulillah* you seem in good health –

*The* USTAZ *steps back in, and the lights change. The scene turns into a explicit pornographic hallucination.* HADIA *repeats her last speech (*'But* elhamdulillah *you seem in good health'*) whilst she makes frantic love to* GASIR *in the* USTAZ'*s bedroom. The* USTAZ *stands there horrified, threatened by the sight of them. He shakes his head and everything returns to normal.*

(*Continuing from before.*) But *elhamdulillah* you seem in good health –

USTAZ (*cutting her off*). I'm sorry, it's the best I can do.

*He points to the container.*

**Scene Nine**

HADIA *is in a lingerie shop, that ranges from the domestic to the naughty, being helped by a female shop* ASSISTANT *who is munching on a sandwich.*

GASIR *is outside the shop by the mannequin display, satisfying his curiosity – like many other men.*

HADIA. Do you have any long nightgowns with a lace bra and panties like Suad Husni's?

ASSISTANT. What are you talking about?

HADIA. From that film *Sunrises and Sunsets*?

ASSISTANT. Oh. (*Bored.*) No!

HADIA. How about this one in purple?

ASSISTANT (*whilst eating*). No.

HADIA. Or something rose-coloured with burgundy flowers?

*The* ASSISTANT *shakes her head: 'No.'*

How about in pink and mauve? Or red and fucshia?

ASSISTANT. No.

HADIA. Are you looking to make some money, or what? Every time I ask you about anything it's, 'No. No.'

ASSISTANT. It's not that… It's just that you come in here every month, and I don't see a wedding ring on your left hand… or on your right. (*Insinuating it might be a forbidden relationship.*) Who you wearing this for?!

HADIA. And what's it to you?! People don't have to wear their wedding rings… (*Pointing at something in the display.*) Do you have that one in my size?

HADIA *notices* GASIR *through the window.*

My God! You see that man standing by the window?

ASSISTANT. Which one?

HADIA. That one wearing glasses...

ASSISTANT. I'm not sure... Which one you talking about? (*Uninterested.*) What's with him, anyway?

HADIA. He's still standing there!!

ASSISTANT. Yes, it happens all the time... So what?

HADIA. 'So what'?! He's looking at us.

ASSISTANT. You know him?

HADIA. Yes, no, but I think he's following me.

ASSISTANT. I don't think so... (*She goes back to eating.*)

HADIA. He's been stalking me, there's no other explanation for it. Why else would he be standing outside a shop where women buy underwear?

ASSISTANT. Look at all the other men standing next to him, waiting to catch a glimpse. I'm telling you, it happens all the time.

HADIA. Oh my God! What is this?! Don't look, don't look!

*She pretends to be browsing, then sneaks a look back to see if* GASIR*'s still there. He is stood there, admiring the mannequins.*

*The scene freezes and turns into a slow-motion sequence from an old black-and-white romantic film.* HADIA *exits the shop to be met by* GASIR *who has been waiting for her. He hands her a rose. They stare into each other's eyes for some time.* HADIA *turns her gaze away in shyness. She shakes her head and everything returns to how it was, except she seems a little angry with herself.*

(*Whispering.*) It's very strange!

ASSISTANT (*mouth full of food*). Nothing's stranger than the devil.

*The scene freezes again.* HADIA *runs, outraged, towards* GASIR. *What follows happens at double speed, as if in a fast-forwarded Woody Allen film.*

HADIA (*exiting the shop*). This is just unbelievable! Don't you have any self-respect?!

GASIR (*in shock*). I was just –

HADIA. You were just what?! It's as clear as day... You're sick!

GASIR. No, please, there's no need for that.

HADIA. You are sick and perverted. A pervert.

GASIR. May God forgive you...

HADIA. May He forgive you for what you're doing to us innocent girls. You filthy man. You're a crazy pervert... Aren't you?

GASIR. I don't understand why you're doing this – But I – My mother – Anyway, I'm sorry.

GASIR *starts to move, he dashes off and a rose falls from him.* HADIA *stands there in disbelief, the* ASSISTANT *watching. Everything returns to how it was.*

ASSISTANT (*rushing her*). Anything else?

HADIA *bolts out of the shop, looking for* GASIR. *She doesn't find him and leaves the stage.*

GASIR *enters from the opposite direction. A moment of doubt hangs in the air. Was he even there to begin with?*

**Scene Ten**

GASIR *is with* THERAPIST 4.

THERAPIST 4. Cast your mind back, to a certain mistake you might've made in the past which upset your mother.

GASIR. What do you mean?

THERAPIST 4. Meaning, did she ever catch you doing something… wrong?

GASIR. Well… Of course, when I was young.

THERAPIST 4. Yes, but what about when you were older?

GASIR. Oh… Once, when I was around sixteen, I'd bought a magazine – off a boy at school, you know.

THERAPIST 4 (*with interest*). So… You were masturbating?

GASIR (*extremely embarrassed*). Yeah.

THERAPIST 4. And then… What happened?

> GASIR's *hand comes to life, as if possessed.* GASIR *battles with it until he pins it down and it subsides.* THERAPIST 4 *doesn't notice.*

GASIR. Nothing…

THERAPIST 4. Nothing what?

GASIR. Nothing… I stopped…

THERAPIST 4. You stopped masturbating?

GASIR. Yes.

THERAPIST 4. Completely?!

GASIR. Yes, *elhamdulillah.*

THERAPIST 4. For good?

GASIR. Yes.

THERAPIST 4. You are a phenomenon, my son... And you're happy this way?

GASIR. No... I'm not happy.

THERAPIST 4. But you're not doing anything about it?

GASIR. What can I do?

THERAPIST 4. Don't you know any girls?

GASIR. No.

THERAPIST 4. At all?

GASIR. No.

THERAPIST 4. The neighbours?

GASIR. No...

THERAPIST 4 (*after a long ponderous thought*). Well, try speaking to one over the phone... Any girl...

*As* THERAPIST 4 *speaks,* GASIR *gets up and heads towards a telephone. He leafs through his phone book until he finds the right number.*

**Scene Eleven**

GASIR *dials a number on his phone, he hesitates a few times then finally goes through with it. The telephone in* USTAZ'*s apartment rings.*

HADIA. Hello.

GASIR. ...

HADIA. Hello, helloooo...

*She puts the phone down.*

GASIR *summons up the courage to call again.*

USTAZ. Hello.

GASIR. …

USTAZ. Helloooo…

GASIR (*low, shy voice*). Hello.

USTAZ. Hello… I can't hear anything, Hadia. Can't hear. See who it is.

*He gives* HADIA *the phone.*

HADIA. Hello.

GASIR *hangs up.*

*He dials again.*

Hello… (*Nervous anticipation.*) Hello.

GASIR (*low*). Hello.

HADIA (*authoritative*). Yes, who am I speaking to?

GASIR *doesn't respond.*

Who is this?

GASIR. Gasir, from Dr Magdi's lab.

HADIA. Yes?

GASIR *tries to speak.*

Yes?

USTAZ. Who is it, Hadia?

HADIA. It's Dr Gasir from the lab.

USTAZ. What does he want?

HADIA. The Ustaz is asking how he can help.

GASIR *tries to say something.* HADIA *is getting bored very quickly.*

GASIR (*suddenly*). When can I come?

*He realises the stupidity of his question.*

HADIA (*surprised*). Excuse me?

GASIR. I mean, when can I come and get that blood sample?

HADIA. He wants to know when he can get that blood sample from you.

USTAZ. Not today, I'm tired…

HADIA (*covering the phone with her hand and scolding him like a child*). Now, we can't keep running away from these tests, can we? The results are delayed already.

USTAZ (*turning away from her*). Fine, fine.

HADIA. What time would be good for you today?

GASIR (*flustered*). Would six be all right?

HADIA. No problem. Bye.

GASIR (*low and romantic*). Bye-bye.

*Blackout as they simultaneously put down their phones.*

## Scene Twelve

HADIA, GASIR *and the* USTAZ *in the apartment, in something very similar to their earlier scene together.*

HADIA. What can I get you to drink?

GASIR *produces the syringe for taking the blood sample.*

USTAZ. How many years has he been doing this?

HADIA. Eight, isn't that right, Dr Gasir?

GASIR *nods his head in agreement.*

USTAZ. Are you Egyptian? You don't look Egyptian.

GASIR. I am.

USTAZ. No, I don't think so. Where are you from?

> GASIR *is still holding the syringe up, waiting for an*
> *opportunity to take the sample.*

GASIR. My family's from Mansoura but I was born here –

HADIA. Where in Mansoura? I'm from Mansoura too.
Mukhtalat or Tureil? Around the new highway, on the out-
skirts?

> GASIR *feels cornered and can't answer.*

Oh, I never got you something to drink. What would you
like?

GASIR. Nothing, thank you.

> *The* USTAZ *has been eyeing both of them.*

USTAZ. You look nervous. Why are you nervous?

> GASIR *prepares to take the sample.* HADIA *rolls up the*
> USTAZ*'s sleeve while* GASIR *searches for a suitable vein.*

No, don't come near me with that thing if you're nervous.
You'll hurt me.

GASIR. But I'm not nervous.

HADIA. Come on, you won't feel a thing. He has delicate
fingers.

USTAZ. No, I have no veins left. I've dried up. Stop looking,
you won't find any.

GASIR. Clench and relax your fist like this…

HADIA. Just like that.

> *She mimics* GASIR.

USTAZ. No, no, no more.

> *He begrudgingly follows her orders. She calms the* USTAZ
> *down to help* GASIR. GASIR*'s attraction to her is apparent.*

GASIR. Yes, clench your fist then relax it, just like that, as if you're squeezing a tomato.

*GASIR places the needle and slowly extracts some blood. The* USTAZ *hangs onto* HADIA, *biting his fist in exaggeration.*

*The lights change and the* USTAZ's *head drops, as if he's been drugged.* GASIR *lets out an evil laugh and* HADIA *looks at him with lust in her eyes. She checks to see if the* USTAZ *is indeed knocked out. Suddenly, the* USTAZ *wakes up and everything goes back to normal.*

HADIA. You sure you wouldn't like something to drink?

GASIR. Thank you.

*He pulls the needle out and empties the syringe into a small vial.*

HADIA. It's not right. We can't have you come round and not have something to drink. We've got some juice if you like? Nothing fizzy unfortunately. Maybe some tea? Or coffee? Turkish? Italian? Or maybe American? We have some Nescafé, if you like. Or maybe you're the healthy type? We've got some herbs. Want some herbal tea?

GASIR. Thank you.

*He searches for something to say.* HADIA *and the* USTAZ *wait for him to speak.*

*Silence.*

USTAZ. Do you want another urine sample?

GASIR. No, thank you.

HADIA. You sure you don't want to drink anything?

GASIR. Thanks.

*Silence.*

May I use the toilet?

HADIA. First on the right…

*We see* GASIR *escape into the bathroom.*

USTAZ (*whispering*). He looks like one of those…

HADIA (*whispering*). What do you mean?

USTAZ (*whispering*). Those homosexuals.

HADIA. How can you tell?

USTAZ. It's obvious. I've seen a few in my time.

HADIA. But he seems normal to me…

USTAZ (*terrified*). You mean, you think he's good enough?

HADIA. For what?

USTAZ. For you… for your mother. So she doesn't send you back to Mansoura.

HADIA. Who knows…

### Scene Thirteen

HADIA *and* GASIR *are on the phone.*

HADIA. Hello.

GASIR. Hello.

HADIA. Evening. Dr Gasir?

GASIR. Yes, good evening –

HADIA. It's Hadia, the assistant of Ustaz Idris.

GASIR. Yes, I know –

HADIA. You know? What do you mean?

GASIR. I mean… How can I help?

HADIA. I'm calling to ask about those tests.

GASIR. Yes, we should have the results in by tomorrow, *Inshallah*.

HADIA. Oh, that long –

GASIR. Should I bring them to you? (*Tries to seem less eager.*) Or you could come by and get them if that's easier – (*Hesitates.*) or maybe someone can pick them up and bring them over... or I could meet you somewhere and give them to you, while you're out with your friends, for example?

HADIA. I've only got my friend Amani. She just had a baby and doesn't go out any more. But could I pick them up from you, while you're out with your friends?

GASIR. Well, unfortunately I don't have any... I don't go out.

HADIA (*takes it as a personal rejection*). I see.

GASIR. I did have one friend, but he emigrated to Canada.

HADIA (*interested*). Seriously? Do you never go out?

GASIR. There is a place... I possibly used to go to...

HADIA. Really...?

GASIR. Yes... Possibly –

HADIA. What?

GASIR. I mean, we could...

HADIA. Yes?

GASIR. Possibly...

HADIA (*to herself*). God give me patience...

USTAZ. Who are you speaking to, Hadia?

HADIA. Yes, I'm coming. (*To* GASIR.) Quickly, where?

USTAZ. Hadia!

GASIR *panics.*

HADIA. Look, hurry up. We could have lemonade on the Nile, maybe sit on the Corniche with our backs to the road? Or go for a walk? I hope you're not the McDonald's type.

GASIR (*not sure what to say*). The supermarket.

HADIA. What? The supermarket?

GASIR. Yes...

HADIA. Why the supermarket?

GASIR (*dejected*). You don't want to?

HADIA. No, no – which one?

GASIR. Sorry?

USTAZ. Hadia!

HADIA. Which supermarket?

GASIR. The big one in Al Agooza.

USTAZ. I think I've neglected my sweet tooth for far too long.

HADIA. Okay, bye.

GASIR. Wait... What time?

USTAZ. Hadia, where did you hide those Turkish Delights?

HADIA. At six. Bye.

**Scene Fourteen**

*The supermarket. HADIA and GASIR in separate aisles, they seem nervous. GASIR spots HADIA but pretends not to have noticed her. He continues browsing, trying to gather up the courage to speak to her. HADIA sees him and waits to see if he approaches. It's a cat-and-mouse game, instigated by HADIA, which leads to them reaching for the same shelf.*

HADIA. Pssst. Don't we know each other? I know we met at the Ustaz's apartment, right? Don't think I'm flirting with you – but we have met before that, right? Here maybe? No – I remember – the spice shop – I'm sorry – Do you normally come here?

GASIR (*lowering his voice*). No problem...

HADIA. I normally come here too...

GASIR (*handing her an envelope*). The results.

HADIA. Thank you. (*Looking in his shopping basket.*) So, you like your nuts?

GASIR. Sorry?

HADIA. I mean, do you like to cook? Or do you have a thing for nuts? You're buying nuts to put in your food, you must be a good cook. What's this? It's mostly fruit and vegetables. Are you on a diet? A vegetarian maybe? Or stomach problems? Everyone I know suffers from irritable bowels, men and women. I believe it's the plague of our times. Don't you think?

GASIR. Possibly.

HADIA. Isn't it a strange coincidence that we've seen each other twice already, even though we've never officially met? And we might never have met. What's the population of Cairo these days? How many people are in Egypt, anyway? What are the chances?! Do you read the newspapers? Because I stopped reading newspapers two years ago, a waste of time, nothing but lies and gossip. For what...? (*Noticing another thing in his basket.*) Oh, it's a good thing you drink milk!

GASIR *feels cornered.*

It's embarrassing how the market is saturated with imports. Barely any Egyptian products. Don't you hate it when they say non-Egyptian is cheaper and better?

GASIR. Hmm...

HADIA. I don't mean to pry, but it's not every day you meet someone you have so much in common with – Do you think you could cook and read poetry to me? I mean, do you think you could cook for your wife? And read poetry to her? Or cook and read poetry together. No, I mean, at the same time…

GASIR *doesn't know what to say.*

Sorry, I'm rambling, and getting a little too personal. Just forget everything I've said.

*Silence. They both distract themselves with the products they've picked up.*

GASIR (*in a low voice*). I like poetry and cooking.

HADIA (*smiling wide*). Me too…

*Nervous silence. Each is about to say something,* HADIA *blurts out first.*

You do like girls, right?

GASIR (*surprised*). Sorry?!

HADIA. I didn't mean to. The Ustaz said… I mean… You like gills… on fish? You like fish, right? Fish.

*Long uncomfortable silence.*

GASIR. Fish in a dish or aquarium fish?

HADIA *smiles.*

HADIA. Both?

GASIR. Oh yes, very much.

*They exchange shy smiles.*

**Scene Fifteen**

GASIR *in his kitchen. He has some books open in front of him as he tries to find a suitable poem.*

HADIA, *at the* USTAZ'*s house, reads an 'advice for brides on their wedding day' book.*

*The* USTAZ *is in another room.*

HADIA *has a chest filled with sexy lingerie, all fiery colours. She practises her hobby of holding up each piece, admiring it, and carefully folding it back whilst reciting from the book in an effort to memorise the advice.*

*They read together simultaneously.*

GASIR.
>Come, love, let us live in an untrodden desert,
>In some shadowy vale, where runs a rivulet,
>Let us go back to our youth and children's madness,
>To the dreams of safety and soundness,
>Oh, Layla, how I long for your lips to meet mine,
>As when lovebirds their beaks entwine,
>To taste of that kiss which makes weak my misery,
>On your lips I feel every blessing, every ecstasy,
>The heart then beats so hard in the chest,
>As though another heart shared with it a single breast.

HADIA. One. On the wedding night, the wife must never behave in a way which makes her husband feel belittled, unworthy, or unsuitable for her needs. Two. If the husband fails her in bed, the wife must convince him that he is at the height of his sexual prowess, despite his failure. Three. The groundwork of flirting and foreplay must be laid down before intercourse between the husband and wife takes place.

USTAZ. Hadia! What time is it?

>GASIR *tries his hand at the difficult task of cooking while reciting the poetry.*

GASIR.

>Oh, Layla, how I long for your lips to meet mine,
>As when lovebirds their beaks entwine,
>To taste of that kiss which makes weak my misery –

HADIA. On the wedding night, the wife must never behave in a way which makes her husband feel belittled, unworthy, or unsuitable for her needs.

*She whispers the sentence again.*

GASIR.

>On your lips I feel every blessing, every ecstasy,
>The heart then beats so hard in the chest,
>As though another heart shared with it a single breast.

HADIA. Two. If the husband fails her in bed, the wife must convince him that he is at the height of his sexual prowess, despite his failure – Why all this pessimism...? We'll just forget about that one...

USTAZ. Hadia! What are you doing, Hadia??

GASIR (*with sudden enthusiasm*).

>Come, love, let us live in an untrodden desert,
>In some shadowy vale, where runs a rivulet,
>Let us go back to our youth and children's madness,
>To the dreams of safety and soundness –

HADIA. Three. The ground work of flirting and foreplay must be laid down before intercourse between the husband and wife takes place.

*She smiles and repeats the sentence in an audible whisper, as if having an orgasm.* GASIR *speaks as she whispers. He takes his mother's gown and places it in the suitcase. He sits on the suitcase closing it shut, feeling very accomplished. A post-coital smile on his face.*

GASIR.

>Oh, Layla, how I long for your lips to meet mine,
>As when lovebirds their beaks entwine –

*The* USTAZ *comes in, surprising* HADIA.

USTAZ. What are you reading?

## Scene Sixteen

GASIR *and* HADIA *are in a restaurant, seated next to an aquarium.*

HADIA. Whenever I'd pass this place, I'd wish I was sitting in here with someone – my fiancé, for example, or my boyfriend... when he became my fiancé, of course. Are you always this quiet?

GASIR. No, I'm listening.

HADIA. Oh, you poor thing. No problem, let's start over.

*She gets up and leaves, then comes back in with a smile on her face.*

Excuse me, is this seat free?

GASIR. Yes.

HADIA (*instructing him*). You mean, I can join you?

*She sits and waits for him to start a conversation, but he remains silent.*

That didn't go too well. Are you bored?

GASIR (*eagerly*). No, no. You?

HADIA. Not at all. Although I do bore easily –

*Just as she is about to launch into another verbal haemorrhage,* GASIR *speaks up bravely.*

GASIR. Do we have to talk?

HADIA. Oh, I get it. You'll look into my eyes, and I'll look into yours. You'll tell me you like me and would like to know me better. I'll play hard-to-get but fall for you in the end. You do like me, don't you?

GASIR. Uh... Yes.

HADIA. Do you have a speech impediment? Maybe a lisp?

GASIR. What?

HADIA. Are you speaking softly so your lisp doesn't show?

GASIR. No –

HADIA. Speak, don't be shy. A lisp can be attractive, sometimes.

GASIR. But I don't have a lisp.

HADIA. So, you're a little slow? Have you never been out with a girl before?

GASIR. I don't know – I'm not sure... Sorry, I need the toilet.

HADIA. Me too.

*We see them enter separate toilets.* GASIR *sits on the toilet seat, fully clothed, hiding from the situation.* HADIA *'powders her nose', checks her phone and fiddles with her veil. They both leave the toilets at the same time.*

*They sit at the table, each waiting for the other to speak.*

Don't you want to tell me something?

GASIR. No...

HADIA. You sure?

GASIR (*after some thought*). What's your star sign?

HADIA. Leo... And you?

GASIR. Libra.

HADIA. I see...

*Silence.*

Don't you have anything else you'd like to say to me?

GASIR. I don't know… Like what?

HADIA. Like what you think of the restaurant.

GASIR. It's nice.

HADIA. Or would you have preferred someplace else? I like it here because of the fish tank.

GASIR. It's nice here.

*Long silence.*

HADIA. Nothing else to say to me then?

*Silence.*

GASIR. I don't know…

*Very long silence.*

HADIA. I think if we meet again tomorrow, maybe we'll be more used to each other by then.

*She leaves.* GASIR *is dumbfounded.*

### Scene Seventeen

GASIR *enters the toilet. He checks his phone a few times.*

*Time passes.*

HADIA *comes back to the apartment and sits next to the* USTAZ. *She flicks through a bridal-fashion magazine and checks her phone every now and again. She gets disheartened and frustrated by the lack of messages. The* USTAZ *watches her, then speaks.*

USTAZ. Don't you want to read me some poetry?

HADIA (*uninterested*). Whatever you like. Who would you like us to read?

USTAZ. How about we watch telly!

HADIA. Fine.

USTAZ. Isn't it time for that Turkish soap opera you've been following? What about that Lebanese game show you like?

*HADIA doesn't answer, reaches for the remote and turns on the television.*

Is something upsetting you?

HADIA. No...

USTAZ. You are upset about something. I can see the suffering in your eyes...

*HADIA is silent.*

Have you made another one run away?

HADIA. No.

*Short silence.*

You think I make them run?

*Her eyes well up and she begins to sob. The USTAZ is surprised by this.*

USTAZ. No, I was only joking. That was a little uncalled for, wasn't it? I'm sorry.

HADIA. Every joke has some truth behind it. I probably do make them run away.

USTAZ. No, they're just not right for you.

HADIA. Why?

USTAZ. They're not worthy of you.

HADIA. I'm not so sure about that.

USTAZ. I just wanted to know where all this sadness is coming from. Any news? Did your mother call again?

HADIA. No.

USTAZ. What then?

*He ponders the situation then becomes anxious.*

I know… The doctor must've called and told you that I'm dying!

HADIA (*half-smiling*). No, don't worry.

USTAZ. So you're not crying over my latest X-ray?

HADIA. No.

USTAZ. Or my blood test?

HADIA. No.

USTAZ. Urine test?

HADIA. No. I read you the results already and everything's fine.

USTAZ. Yes, yes. So, what is it? What's wrong?

HADIA. I'm just in a foul mood…

USTAZ. Yes, but why? Are you in love? Tell me.

HADIA *shakes her head.*

Just tell me. I don't understand…

HADIA. I'm in foul mood, that's all.

USTAZ. I understand. I'll help you. I'll speak to him. Hmm? It's the one who did my tests, isn't it?

HADIA *shakes her head again, disagreeing with his assumption, although slightly surprised by his perceptiveness.*

I understand. Tell me.

HADIA. I'm sorry, I don't want to talk about it…

HADIA *pulls the curtain between herself and* USTAZ, *separating the bedroom.*

GASIR *goes back home. He hangs his mother's dress up and starts to cook.*

### Scene Eighteen

GASIR *and* HADIA *in their separate spaces between a chest of dreams, a kitchen, and a toilet.*

HADIA. I can't really describe the man of my dreams, I mean, what he looks like doesn't matter to me. Like you for example, you're particularly not handsome –

GASIR. Your name's Hadia, but you're not a calm one, although you do make me laugh. I haven't had much to laugh about since Mama died –

HADIA. And your voice isn't very masculine.

GASIR. But still that isn't enough somehow...

HADIA. I'll try to be calmer the next time we meet... and let you do the talking.

GASIR. I don't talk much – You could be a little more sensitive, though...

HADIA. Fine, I'll try to be like the rest of the girls, all shy and embarrassed.

GASIR. This isn't going to work unless you're patient with me...

HADIA (*sudden anger*). Well, you're not helping either...

GASIR. I hate cruelty.

HADIA. You need to learn how to speak up and say something, and your voice – the voice is very important. Your voice should be a little louder –

GASIR. I know –

HADIA. Louder than mine at least...

GASIR. I know you're the type who thinks I'm weak. You won't respect me –

HADIA. Well, you seem like the type who's afraid of what people say.

GASIR. I don't want a girl to embarrass me in front of others.

HADIA. No, no, I want a man who doesn't waste a million years twiddling his thumbs, waiting for me to speak.

GASIR. The thing I hate the most is when someone puts me down for my romanticism and lack of speaking –

HADIA. Anyway, I wanted a man who's tall and broad, with tanned skin and green eyes…

GASIR. I can't say you're not pretty –

HADIA. Nothing like you.

GASIR. But beauty isn't everything.

HADIA. And I noticed you have small feet!

GASIR. There's something attractive about you, but you talk too much…

HADIA. You say, I say, makes no difference to me.

GASIR. And that is slightly unacceptable.

HADIA. I just want a baby…

GASIR. I've always wanted someone to share everything with: the cooking, the poetry, and the children. Someone to wake up next to me.

HADIA (*she thinks then shakes her head*). No, no, this won't work at all, I'm too strong for him.

GASIR. It's a shame that's so difficult to find.

THERAPIST 4 *suddenly appears*.

THERAPIST 4. Gasir, my son, remember that weakness is unacceptable. Whenever you find yourself hiding from the world, take a leap and just express yourself. No one will judge you for what you say, my son, say what you feel and venture forth, venture forth! Don't look at life through a keyhole, open that door, and start living!

GASIR, *overcome with confidence, takes his phone and dials. The phone rings in the* USTAZ's *apartment.*

USTAZ. Hadia…

   HADIA *rushes in.*

HADIA. Hello… (*She frowns in disappointment.*)

USTAZ. So…

HADIA. *W'allaikum essallam.*

USTAZ. Is it that lab assistant?

HADIA (*very depressed*). *Elhamdulillah*, and how are you
   Mama?

USTAZ. Hmm, I guess it's not that lab assistant.

HADIA (*with a mixture of frustration and insistence*). No.
   Nothing new, Mama.

### Scene Nineteen

*Another day – Another place – Another situation.*

HADIA. Do you come here often?

GASIR. Not really.

HADIA. Alone? Or do you sit with someone else?

GASIR. Sometimes I sit alone… sometimes – well, a while ago
   – with my friend… I used to come here with my mother too,
   God rest her soul…

HADIA. What do you normally do here?

GASIR. Sometimes I read, and other times I sit quietly,
   watching people go by.

HADIA. Don't you ever want to be like the people sitting
   around you?

GASIR. How?

HADIA. I mean, wouldn't you like to sit here with your girl-friend, or fiancée, for example?

GASIR *is silent*.

Why aren't you talking?

GASIR. I'm thinking.

HADIA. Of what?

GASIR. Of Mama, God rest her soul, when we used to read the Abir Chronicles – you know, the love stories – and long for the day I would be sitting here with a girl…

HADIA. Abir Chronicles, *The Immortal Love*, that kind of thing? You used to read those soppy romance novels? Why?

GASIR (*embarrassed*). What's wrong with that?

HADIA. 'What's wrong with that'?! I stopped reading those when I was fourteen. Even then I was embarrassed to be reading them. Don't tell me you also read *Roses*, the Egyptian edition?!

GASIR. I don't like your attitude…

HADIA. Never mind, I'm sorry. Sorry…

GASIR *has taken it personally*.

Have you never had a girlfriend before?

GASIR. No.

HADIA. Why?

GASIR. Uh, too busy.

HADIA. With what?

GASIR. I can't really say.

HADIA. Please. Tell me, otherwise I'll worry.

GASIR. No, there's nothing to worry about. The thing is, I was taking care of my mother for the past few years because of her illness.

HADIA. Aww… (*To herself.*) But this way I won't be able to get jealous. (*Worried.*) Aren't you the jealous type?

GASIR. Why should I be jealous?

HADIA. Excuse me?! Don't you intend to marry me?

GASIR. Sorry? But we're getting to know each other.

HADIA. Yes, but don't think I'm the type to play the field, hopping from one man to the next. No, no, I'm not piling up my trousseau for that. I shouldn't even be here with you! Don't you dare think I'm a girl you can kiss and grope on the Corniche! No, no, no! Wake up and smell the coffee! I'm a woman who demands respect. I wear my veil on the inside as well. My modesties are covered inside and out.

GASIR. I'm sorry, but I never suggested otherwise…

HADIA. Excuse me?! That's all that's missing! All my previous relationships have been virtuous, the most we ever did was hold hands, in case your mind starts to wander.

GASIR. Have there been many previous relationships?

HADIA (*quietens down, ignores his question*). I wouldn't even accept a temporary marriage, and I have been asked. My pride wouldn't allow it.

GASIR. Temporary? I'm sure… But you are a romantic, aren't you?

HADIA. What do you mean?

GASIR. I mean, we could talk on the phone, watch romantic films and write each other love letters… Couldn't we?

HADIA. Love letters?

GASIR. Yes, when one of us travels… Did I say something wrong?

HADIA. No, not at all. I'm just taking it in.

GASIR. Does what I'm saying seem strange to you?

HADIA. No, not necessarily.

GASIR (*to himself*). The doctor said I have to let go and be myself.

HADIA. Doctor?!

GASIR. Sorry, I need the toilet.

HADIA. Hang on, I'm talking to you… What doctor?

GASIR (*ignoring the question*). Sorry, I'm going to the toilet.

HADIA. If you go to the toilet again, I'm leaving!

GASIR. Sorry?

HADIA. I said, if you go to the toilet one more time, I'm leaving.

GASIR. Why? Everyone has to go to the toilet, don't they?

HADIA. Yes, but not everyone has to see a 'doctor'.

GASIR. And there are people who need to see a doctor but don't.

HADIA (*insulted*). Excuse me? Are you implying something?

GASIR. I'm going to the toilet.

HADIA. And I'm leaving!

GASIR. You're behaving very strangely.

HADIA. Excuse me?! Are you doubting my upbringing?

GASIR. Sorry?

HADIA (*threatening*). I'm leaving…

GASIR (*with sadness*). And I'm going to the toilet.

HADIA *can't believe he has walked off. She leaves, angry, her pride injured.*

### Scene Twenty

GASIR *in various positions onstage: in the toilet, in the kitchen, in empty space. He rings* HADIA.

HADIA *in various positions onstage: in the* USTAZ's *bedroom, with her chest of dreams, in empty space. Her phone rings, she hesitates but never answers.*

HADIA *looks at her phone as it rings.*

USTAZ. Aren't you going to answer that?

HADIA. No.

USTAZ. Are you sure?

HADIA. Yes.

USTAZ. Why not?

*Pause.*

HADIA (*shrugging her shoulders*). You think I should?

USTAZ. It's up to you.

HADIA. No, I won't. I have to be strong.

USTAZ. You're right... It's better this way...

HADIA. Yeah... Maybe.

USTAZ. What if he rings again?

HADIA. I don't know.

USTAZ. Go on, answer it.

HADIA. It's stopped now.

USTAZ. Why don't you call him?

HADIA. No.

USTAZ. Ah, you don't want him to think you're chasing after him? (*After some time.*) But he is kind, that Gasir.

HADIA (*sadly*). Yeah...

**Scene Twenty-One**

HADIA *in various positions onstage: in the* USTAZ*'s bedroom, in the toilet, in empty space.*

*She rings* GASIR.

GASIR *in various positions onstage: in the kitchen, in the toilet, in empty space. He sees that it's* HADIA *calling. He hesitates but never answers.*

USTAZ. He's still not answering?

HADIA. Who?

USTAZ (*teasing her*). Mr Medical Tests…

HADIA. I wasn't calling him…

USTAZ. Who else could it be?

HADIA. No one.

USTAZ. No. I know.

HADIA. I told you, it's nobody.

USTAZ. I know who you're calling.

HADIA. That's impossible. Who is it then?

USTAZ. Both of us know who it is.

HADIA. I have no idea what you're talking about.

USTAZ. That's all right, as long as I know.

HADIA (*pissed off*). Fine, you know.

## Scene Twenty-Two

*The* USTAZ *is dictating to* HADIA. *She writes down his words.*

USTAZ. Lina was my first love, she was my last…

HADIA. Are you sure about that? I don't think that's true.

USTAZ. How would you know?

HADIA. You told me. I remember you saying that the woman you loved the most was Mirvat who died of cancer. Remember?

USTAZ (*slyly*). I don't remember…

HADIA. Well, I do…

*Silence.*

*The phone rings. From her reaction, we know it's* GASIR.

USTAZ. Speak to the medical-test man.

HADIA (*overeager*). Why?

USTAZ. So he can come and bring the new test results.

HADIA. But the results aren't in yet. I'm sure Dr Magdi will send them over himself when they're ready.

USTAZ. No… I want that Gasir to come.

HADIA. Why him?! I thought you didn't like him.

USTAZ. No, that's not true! Call him.

HADIA. There's no need.

USTAZ. Well then, give me the phone and I'll call him.

HADIA. No. There's no need.

USTAZ. Have you two had a fight?!

HADIA. There was nothing there to fight about!

USTAZ. Give me the telephone.

HADIA. No.

USTAZ. Are you trying to control me?!

HADIA (*helplessly*). No...

USTAZ. What then? I don't understand why you're so against me giving him a call. I'm sure something's happened between you two.

HADIA. Sort of...

USTAZ. I knew it. What did you fight about? So... Was he rude to you? Did he try anything?

HADIA. No.

USTAZ. He turned out to be a homosexual?! I knew it!

HADIA. Not at all.

USTAZ. Well, what then?

HADIA. He's seeing a psychiatrist...

USTAZ. What's wrong with that? That's quite normal these days.

HADIA. No, it's not normal.

USTAZ. Is that what you said to him?

HADIA. Yes!

USTAZ. No, no, you had no right to.

HADIA. But he was also implying things about my reputation and upbringing.

USTAZ. Gasir? I don't believe it... Why would he do that?

HADIA. Because I have more experience than he does!

USTAZ. You've had quite a few, haven't you?

*She ignores the question.*

And he hasn't?

HADIA. No.

USTAZ. Are you sure he's not a homosexual? They're a fiercely jealous people.

HADIA (*annoyed*). Yes, I'm sure.

USTAZ. Yes, yes, I am sure of it too. He couldn't possibly be one.

HADIA *gives him a dismissive look.*

The only logical explanation is that he's jealous, because you haven't been massaging his ego… (*He makes a gesture with his hands, as if tickling a little girl.*)

HADIA (*laughing in spite of herself*). How am I supposed to do that?

USTAZ. What are any of us supposed to do? People are just horrible these days, jealous and envious. No one has a sense of loyalty any more. Bring me the phone. I'll take care of it.

HADIA. No!

USTAZ. Fine, it's his loss. He doesn't deserve someone like you, anyway. I don't like his male-chauvinist attitude.

HADIA. Oh, really?! Weren't you exactly the same when you were his age?

USTAZ (*innocently*). Me?

HADIA. Why didn't you marry 'Lina' then?

USTAZ. Oh, Hadia, now I've got a headache. Where are those painkillers? Why do you have to bring these things up now? Lina is dead and I'm going to follow her soon. I was an idiot. What else do you want me to say?

HADIA. You're not helping.

USTAZ. Don't worry, you'll be in my will. I'll leave you some money.

HADIA. I'm not talking about money, I'm talking about my life.

USTAZ. I'm talking about dying and all you can think about is your life. So selfish. Just like my daughter.

HADIA. I'm sorry, I didn't meant to.

USTAZ. Fine, now get me Gasir on the phone.

HADIA. No.

*She leaves the room.*

USTAZ (*shouting after her*). You'll be sorry when I'm dead.

## Scene Twenty-Three

*The* USTAZ's *apartment.* GASIR *stands in front of* HADIA, *holding a pot of food he has cooked. He stutters, not making sense of what he recites.*

GASIR.
> Although she is now distant,
> Her beauty in my heart persistent,
> If the heart brims over then why –
> Does it ache when no trace of her is nigh?

HADIA. Excuse me?

GASIR (*rushing*). All right...
> You are far, yet close in my sweet torment,
> My eyes and heart lament,
> You I have loved, that for me is sufficient.

HADIA (*in a cold and formal tone*). Welcome.

GASIR (*with a great deal of effort*). How are you?

HADIA (*she signals for him to sit down*). Please.

GASIR. Good evening...

USTAZ (*with a cunning smile*). Evening. How dare you come here again?!

HADIA *shoots him a sharp look and he changes his tone.*

What a pleasant surprise! Are you here to see me?

GASIR. I came to give you the test results, and, of course, to see you too, Ustaz.

USTAZ. You're very kind. What's that you've got there?

GASIR (*trying to hide the pot of food*). Oh, it's nothing – I mean, it's for you.

USTAZ. So, what's the news?

GASIR. Let's see. Your sugar, urea, and creatine levels are a little high. White blood cell count is lower than it should be –

USTAZ. As usual. Hadia will compare them to my previous results.

GASIR. If she needs any help, I could…

HADIA (*objecting*). Thank you. I'm used to going over them with Dr Magdi.

USTAZ. Would you like a drink, my son?

GASIR. I'm fine, thank you.

HADIA. Maybe some milk?

USTAZ. Why milk?

GASIR (*shyly*). I'm rather fond of milk, actually…

USTAZ. Milk!

*A long embarrassing silence.*

**Scene Twenty-Four**

USTAZ. She's still not answering? Call her again.

HADIA. She won't answer, she's at work. People tend not to answer when they're busy at work.

USTAZ. I'll start telling people my daughter has left me, she emigrated. It's over! She's gone! I can't even lean over to put on my own socks. My whole body aches and grinds. I want to rip it off me... This old horse has finally keeled over. It's over...

*He complains, not noticing* HADIA's *miserable expression.*

HADIA (*frustrated*). All this because she won't answer?

USTAZ. You want to desert me too. There is no loyalty... No one appreciates the value of hard work... No honesty...

HADIA. Me?! I don't have any loyalty? Me?!

*She is truly hurt.*

USTAZ (*softening*). No, not you specifically... The others out there, everyone else. The human race... Including you! Don't you want to get married, and leave me?!

HADIA. No more marriage! That's it, I don't want to get married! Enough!

*She starts to cry.*

USTAZ. Are you upset?

HADIA (*blowing her nose*). No.

USTAZ. Don't be upset. I'll dedicate my next book to you.

HADIA. I'm not upset with you.

USTAZ. No?

HADIA. No, I'm upset with myself... I'm pathetic.

USTAZ (*extremely surprised*). What's this? Why?

HADIA. Just because.

USTAZ. But why?

HADIA. I've put him off.

USTAZ. Yes, but why?

HADIA. I don't know! He scared me all of a sudden.

USTAZ (*in disbelief*). Gasir?!

HADIA. He didn't deserve for me to speak to him like that.

USTAZ. Ah, I felt it. We were both so rude to him... Never mind... I'll make it up to him, get him a present. I'll give him a signed copy of my new book.

HADIA (*suddenly bursting with emotion*). I don't know what to do. I'm so confused. I've put him off. He's had enough of me now. That's it.

USTAZ. Do you love him?

HADIA. Maybe I do love him... maybe I just like him, I don't know. Maybe I'm feeling this way because I'm at a crisis and –

USTAZ. Crisis?

HADIA. Yes, I'm almost thirty and I want to have a baby! I don't want to go back to Mansoura! I want to find someone just like me! Someone who loves me, who I can love back – and who loves you, of course.

*The* USTAZ *smiles.*

I don't know what to do any more... I don't know... Nobody loves me. Why doesn't anybody love me? Why is it so hard for someone to love me?

USTAZ. I love you.

*Awkward silence.*

Now, tell me what the problem is.

HADIA. I've put him off.

USTAZ. Who? Which one?

HADIA. Have there been that many?

*She starts to cry again.*

USTAZ. No, I remember. I remember. Gasir. It's simple. Call him and tell him everything you've told me. I'm sure he'll understand.

HADIA. Of course not... I'm sure he's sick of me, anyway.

## Scene Twenty-Five

GASIR *listens to 'Bitmoot [She Dies]' from the Ziad Rahbani album,* Monodose. *He takes his mother's dresses and gowns out of the suitcase. He sings along with the song.*

HADIA *is in the* USTAZ's *bedroom, alone and dressed in black. She has a travel case that she places her things into. She seems lost. There is a taped reading of the Qur'an playing in the background. The phone rings and she answers it.*

HADIA (*on the phone*). Hello... Hello...

GASIR *is on the other end, he listens but doesn't answer.*

(*A little desperate.*) Hello... Hello?

GASIR. Uh...

HADIA (*on the phone, hopefully*). Hello... Hello... Hello...

GASIR *starts to speak, but holds back. He seems sad and pained.*

Hello, who is this? (*On the verge of crying.*) Hello, Hello...

GASIR *starts to cry. He puts the phone down so she can't hear him.*

HADIA *sits on the travel case, in between the phone and the* USTAZ's *empty chair.*

## Scene Twenty-Six

*The supermarket.* HADIA *browsing through the aisles. She takes her time reading the labels on the products.*

GASIR *enters, pushing a shopping trolley. He sees* HADIA. *Not sure what to do, he pretends not to have noticed her.*

*We realise* HADIA *has been waiting for him. She approaches him slowly, in an attempt to surprise him.*

HADIA. Do you speak Bulgarian? I didn't frighten you, did I? How are you? You looked like you were daydreaming.

GASIR *shakes his head: 'No.'*

Yes, I did frighten you. I'm sorry, it's just that I can't read Bulgarian… Can you read Bulgarian?

GASIR (*surprised*). No.

HADIA. There just aren't any good sugar-free juices that are made in Egypt any more. The Ustaz has to – I mean, he had to – have sugar-free juice – you know.

GASIR. I'm sorry, I didn't send you my condolences. I know how you feel…

HADIA. Imagine, they haven't translated the packaging. Does this look sugar-free to you?

GASIR. I don't know.

HADIA (*after some silence*). You see, I try to buy Egyptian products, but it's difficult sometimes.

*Silence.*

Do you boycott?

GASIR (*surprised*). Sorry?

HADIA. I try to, but never manage it – Nothing bothers me as much as all those products they make in the Gulf. Their governments subsidise these awful exports, and we buy into it. Can you believe it?! My mum buys them, unfortunately. We're always fighting about it. Does your mother buy them?

GASIR. No. I mean, before she passed away, God bless her, they weren't as available…

HADIA. Oh yes, I forgot.

GASIR. It's all right, no problem.

*He pretends to be interested in the product he's holding.*

How are you holding up?

*A sad smile crosses her face, she shakes her head: 'I'm fine.'*

If you ever need anything…

*Silence, as they avert each other's gaze.*

*The scenes changes suddenly, as if in a Bollywood movie. GASIR and HADIA dance to the song 'Bitmoot'. The USTAZ joins them and sings along, then disappears.*

*HADIA and GASIR return to the nervousness they were in before.*

*GASIR is about to say something but doesn't. The silence continues. HADIA tries to hide her disappointment.*

HADIA. I forgot to ask you something the last time –

*Silence.*

*GASIR looks at her with anticipation.*

(*Quickly.*) Will you marry me?

*GASIR is gobsmacked and cannot react at all, which only deepens HADIA's disappointment. She is vulnerable and embarrassed but tries to control herself.*

(*Suddenly.*) Do you support Egyptian products?

GASIR. Sorry?

HADIA. Egyptian products. Do you support them?

GASIR. *Ya'ni…* Sure…

HADIA. I've started to think that it doesn't really matter…
Egyptian or not, it's all the same.

Right?

*The End.*